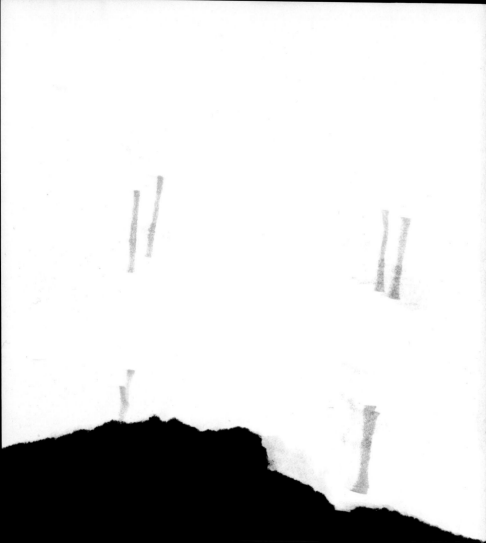

Why Conservative
Churches
Are Growing

Why Conservative Churches Are Growing

A Study in Sociology of Religion

Dean M. Kelley

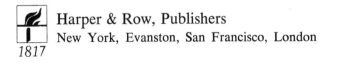
Harper & Row, Publishers
New York, Evanston, San Francisco, London
1817

Figures 1–5 and 15 have been adapted from graphs originally appearing in *Historical Atlas of Religion in America* by Edwin Scott Gaustad, Harper & Row, 1962. Used by permission of the publisher.

LIBRARY OF CONGRESS CATALOG CARD NUMBER: 77-175156

Contents

Preface

The purpose of this book is to clear up some of the existing confusion about what can be expected of religion and under what conditions. Because of this confusion, many look for either too little or too much. Those expect too little who think religion a dispensable superstition, distracting men from the real business of life; those hope for too much who think religion should forthwith make men moral, unselfish, courageous, equalitarian, and kind. Both views show a lack of awareness of what religion can (and can't) do, and an even greater misconception of *how* it occasionally achieves the spiritual quickening expected of it.

Many other authors have already written on this subject. Their works embolden this one in three ways: they show there is wide interest in the subject, they display no general consensus but rather great disparity, and they overcomplicate and overintellectualize a common and familiar mode of human behavior.

The reasons why religious undertakings succeed or fail, and what success and failure mean in the religious realm, seem so apparent that it should not be necessary to spell them out, yet widespread and reiterated misconceptions suggest they may not be so obvious to all—or that he who thinks them obvious may be the one mistaken.

1. It is generally assumed that religious enterprises, if they want to succeed, will be reasonable, rational, courteous, responsible, restrained, and receptive to outside criticism; that is, they will want

to preserve a good image in the world (as the world defines all these terms).

2. It is expected, moreover, that they will be democratic and gentle in their internal affairs (again, as the outside world defines these qualities).

3. They will also be responsive to the needs of men (as currently conceived), and will want to work cooperatively with other groups to meet those needs.

4. They will not let dogmatism, judgmental moralism, or obsessions with cultic purity stand in the way of such cooperation and service.

These expectations are a recipe for the failure of the religious enterprise, and arise from a mistaken view of what success in religion is and how it should be fostered and measured. The current indications, cited in Chapters I and II, that all is not well with the hitherto flourishing churches of the United States may provide an incentive to examine some presuppositions about religion which we were not formerly prepared to question. For reasons suggested presently, it is probably too late to prevent or greatly delay the decline in the ecumenical "mainline" denominations, but it may not be too late to achieve a certain wry appreciation of the qualities liberal churchmen have found so objectionable in the nonecumenical, nonmainline church bodies and to encourage them to maintain those qualities.

For precisely the sectarian and theologically conservative religious groups have made amazing gains in recent years. Amid the current neglect and hostility toward organized religion in general, the conservative churches, holding to seemingly outmoded theology and making strict demands on their members, have equalled or surpassed in growth the yearly percentage increases of the nation's population. And while the mainline churches have tried to support the political and economic claims of our society's minorities and outcasts, it is the sectarian groups that have had most success in attracting new members from these very sectors of society. This book is an attempt to explain the function performed by religion and to show how the conservative churches seem to be fulfilling that function to the satisfaction of more and more adherents.

To some, such an undertaking may seem perverse, exposing the ecumenical churches from within to the reproaches of their conservative critics. This volume is not intended to be used as a weapon by one group of churches against another, since they are all subject to the same dynamics, some a little earlier than others. Yet the common mortality of men does not deter them from fighting one another on the way, and it is probably too much to expect that one church will not cite this work against another to say, "We told you so." Nevertheless, if the dynamics it describes are *true,* it is better for all to know them—even to the embarrassment of some —than to persist in vulnerable unawareness.

Some will consider "dying" a needlessly harsh word to use in describing the condition of some churches. It is not meant to be sensational or melodramatic; in a sense all organizations are dying, as are all higher forms of life from the moment of birth. "Life itself is an incurably fatal disease." And some corporate bodies—particularly religious organizations, such as the Parsees—have been expiring for centuries, yet a tiny remnant persists. The longevity of churches is legendary, and even dying ones can be virtually indestructible.

Yet the word is not intended as a trifle or a truism either. It is used instead of "declining" or "ebbing" to suggest that the phenomenon we are seeing is neither cyclical nor adventitious. It refers to a loss of vitality more significant and perhaps more fatal than a temporary lull. It implies a long-term dynamic in the life of organizations, particularly of religious organizations, that is not as readily apparent in empires or corporations that rise and fall.

Recognition of such a dynamic need not plunge us into the "organismic fallacy" of conceiving of corporate structures as having a life of their own that is somehow independent of the individuals who constitute them. Yet organizations do begin, grow, flourish, decrease, and die, presumably as a result of various forces and conditions we only dimly discern and probably cannot soon control. Better understanding of those forces and conditions may help us to conserve the vitality of organizations we do not want to lose.

A final reason for using the word dying is that the process we see at work in the churches is probably not reversible. Having once succumbed to debility, a church is unlikely to recover, not because measures leading to recovery could not be prescribed and instituted (some are suggested in what follows), but because the persons who now occupy positions of leadership and followership in the church will not find them congenial and will not want to institute them. They prefer a church which is not too strenuous or demanding—a church, in fact, which is dying.

This state of affairs is not necessarily a reproach either to leaders or to followers; the leaders of the declining churches include some of the most humane, personable, intelligent, modest, and committed men in the country, whose values and interests are broader and perhaps better than mere devotion to the maintenance of an organization, particularly under the conditions prescribed in what follows for a strong or vigorous religious body. If that is the case, there may be a basic incompatibility between a religious leader (narrowly defined) and a social statesman (a moral opinion-molder for the civic commonwealth). If there *is* such an incompatibility, the sooner we know it the better. We can then correct our expectations of the denominational executive, and he will less often find himself on ambiguous and exposed promontories of public attention. He may also in time acquire more genuine influence and enduring esteem as one who excells in a unique and indispensable service: helping the members of his religious group to make sense of the earthly predicament.

In order to clarify what success and failure mean in the realm of religion, it is necessary to define that realm and what goes on in it, and this is the object of Chapter III. To measure success and failure, a distinctively human scale of effort and effect is developed in Chapter IV. According to that scale, certain religious movements exceed all other human undertakings in significance, and four such movements are described in Chapter V. From the generalized historical pattern of such movements, several conclusions are drawn about what constitutes and maintains strength and vitality in religious organizations, and the remaining chapters attempt to explore the mechanisms by which social strength is conserved.

A set of hypotheses is offered which purports to explain why the churches are in mortal decline. Most of these can be verified empirically but have not been, for lack of time, resources, and facilities. There are many ambitious doctoral candidates looking for handy hypotheses to test through neatly delimited empirical research, but there are fewer efforts to synthesize a theoretical framework that will make intelligible a wide range of previously unrelated or inadequately understood phenomena. This is what is attempted here, in such formulations as can eventually be empirically proved or disproved by others. The risk of being wrong I gladly take, and if these hypotheses are disproved, no one will be more relieved than I.

If Christian churches are dying, why not explain their plight in Christian terms rather than sociological ones? A clergyman convinced that the Christian understanding of reality and man's nature and duty is true might do well to write within that framework rather than trying to generalize to the whole population of religion. I could have written another book saying the same things, based on Christian assumptions and expressed in Christian concepts*— but that book has been written many times by others more qualified, though they differ among themselves in particulars, giving their critics additional justification to discount them. I also might have spelled out my personal system of meaning, but then *that* would have become the object of acceptance or rejection, rather than the broader dynamic of cause and effect which is bringing on the death of the churches irrespective of whether or not they happen to agree with my personal understanding of meaning or any other.

Religious organizations have succeeded splendidly with the most diverse formulations of the significance of life, and I do not want to seem to limit successful religious functioning to past or present Protestant or Christian or even Western traditions. The strength of this stance is that it attempts to appeal to an arguably universal need or interest of humankind, which can be met with varying degrees of effectiveness by many different religious traditions, including perhaps some not yet developed. Its weakness is that it does

---

* As Peter Berger did in *Rumor of Angels* (New York: Doubleday Anchor Books, 1970), written as a Christian commentary on *The Sacred Canopy* (New York: Doubleday Anchor Books, 1967), his prior sociological work.

not do justice to the unique qualities of any one religious system.

A colleague has criticized this as a merely social-pragmatic approach and therefore ultimately false to the distinctive imperative of Christianity. "The Church can never be thought of simply as a religious institution. It bears the Gospel. . . . Churches as institutions are dying precisely because they have become merely religious and turned away from the revelation of God in Christ, the work of God in history, which is to say have lost their grip upon the Gospel, or rather allowed the Gospel to lose its grip upon them. This reliance upon 'religion' seems to me to yield up a social-pragmatic assumption concerning the effectiveness of religious institutions."

Of course, every faith-group considers itself the One True Faith and all others imposters: sects, cults, conventicles, apostasies, heresies, or idolatries. To the degree that it comes to think of itself as one among many similar and equally meritorious others, it has already begun to lose its appeal. But the fact that each thinks itself unique (and is, in many ways) does not in the least make it or any of its rivals less religious. If Christianity is *not* a religion, what is it?

Of course, no one would want to be "merely religious." But it is no easy thing to be an effective religious organization, and the churches are dying today not because they are merely religious but *because they are not very religious at all* (in the sense defined in this book). On the other hand, a Christian church that effectively embodies the views expressed in the quoted paragraph will undoubtedly find itself functioning very powerfully as a religion, whether or not it wants to be so classified. In fact, the more vehemently it insists that it is *not* just another mere religious institution, the more effective it is likely to be in performing the religious function for its members!

Appreciation is expressed to the National Council of Churches for providing a sabbatical leave during which this book could be developed. The General Secretary, Dr. R. H. Edwin Espy, and the Associate General Secretary for Christian Life and Mission, Dr. Jon L. Regier, both generously approved the plan for this study, though the outline suggested that it might not prove entirely congenial to the ecumenical movement.

Appreciation is also expressed to Father Robert Chapman, Executive Director of the Department of Social Justice of the National Council of Churches, to Mrs. Doreen Graves and my other colleagues in that department and elsewhere in the NCC for their continuing help and interest, and most especially to my secretary, Mr. Rufus Egwu Nwogu, whose perceptive and conscientious labors in typing the manuscript have been altogether above and beyond the call of duty.

Why Conservative
Churches
Are Growing

Chapter I

Are the Churches Dying?

In the latter years of the 1960's something remarkable happened in the United States: for the first time in the nation's history most of the major church groups stopped growing and began to shrink. Though not one of the most dramatic developments of those years, it may prove to be one of the most significant, especially for students of man's social behavior. Certainly those concerned with religion, either as adherents or observers, have wondered what it means and what it portends for the future.

At least ten of the largest Christian denominations in the country, whose memberships totaled 77,666,223 in 1967, had fewer members the next year and fewer yet the year after. Most of these denominations had been growing uninterruptedly since colonial times. In the previous decade they had grown more slowly, some failing to keep pace with the increase in the nation's population. And now they have begun to diminish, reversing a trend of two centuries.

The growth in membership of the major church groups in the United States has been reconstructed by Edwin Scott Gaustad in his authoritative *Historical Atlas of Religion in America*.[1] His graphs show varying rates of increase for the several religious "families" from 1800 to 1960, more or less proportionate to the increase of population for that period. Since his work was published,

1. New York: Harper & Row, 1962.

figures have become available for the ensuing decade, and they tell a different story. In each of several main denominational groups the strong upward curve weakens, falters, and tilts downward like a spent skyrocket, as may be seen in the accompanying graphs.

Since the scale of Gaustad's graphs does not lend itself to a clear reporting of the brief period since 1960, a separate graph for 1960–70 follows each of them, magnifying on a different scale the most recent developments in each denomination.

Figures 1a, 1b, and 1c show the Lutheran groups. Gaustad (Fig. 1a) has recorded all Lutherans in the United States, but the enlargement (Fig. 1b) shows the further aggregate growth of the three main Lutheran bodies only: the Lutheran Church in America, the American Lutheran Church, and the Lutheran Church–Missouri Synod. Until 1963, they increased more rapidly than the total U.S. population growth (which was on the average 1.4% for each year of the decade). Then they grew at an uneven but slower pace until in 1969 the aggregate total *decreased*. This is due to the first two bodies, not to the Missouri Synod, which reported a slight increase. The same pattern recurred in 1970. (In 1969, the Lutheran Church in America began to report its Canadian membership separately, so the Canadian membership has been combined with the American membership for 1969 and 1970 in the graph to maintain commensurability with the earlier years of the decade.) Fig. 1c shows the aggregate church school enrollment for the same three Lutheran bodies.

Reports for the years 1960–70 are taken from the respective issues of the *Yearbook of American Churches*, prepared and edited by the National Council of Churches.

Figures 2a, 2b, and 2c represent the Episcopal Church, whose membership leveled off between 1964 and 1967 and then began to drop. As with the Lutherans, this trend was reflected earlier in church school enrollment.

Figures 3a, 3b, and 3c record Methodist membership. Gaustad's graph (Fig. 3a) includes three predominantly black Methodist bodies as well as the three large predominantly white bodies which merged in 1939, and several small Methodist groups. The enlarged

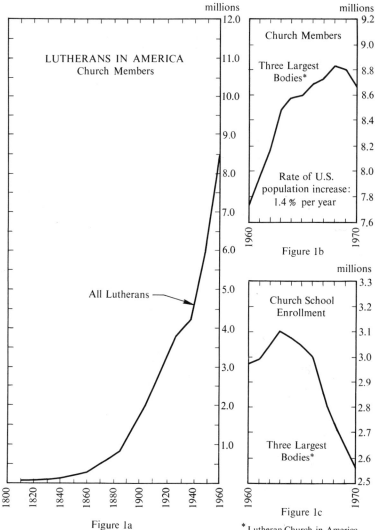

millions

LUTHERANS IN AMERICA
Church Members

All Lutherans ⟶

12.0
11.0
10.0
9.0
8.0
7.0
6.0
5.0
4.0
3.0
2.0
1.0

1800 1820 1840 1860 1880 1900 1920 1940 1960

Figure 1a

millions

Church Members

Three Largest
Bodies*

Rate of U.S.
population increase:
1.4 % per year

9.2
9.0
8.8
8.6
8.4
8.2
8.0
7.8
7.6

1960   1970

Figure 1b

millions

Church School
Enrollment

Three Largest
Bodies*

3.3
3.2
3.1
3.0
2.9
2.8
2.7
2.6
2.5

1960   1970

Figure 1c

* Lutheran Church in America.
American Lutheran Church.
Lutheran Church — Missouri
Synod

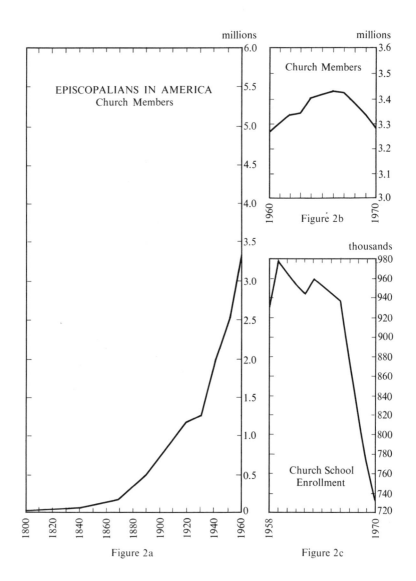

millions

EPISCOPALIANS IN AMERICA
Church Members

millions

Church Members

Figure 2b

thousands

Church School
Enrollment

Figure 2a

Figure 2c

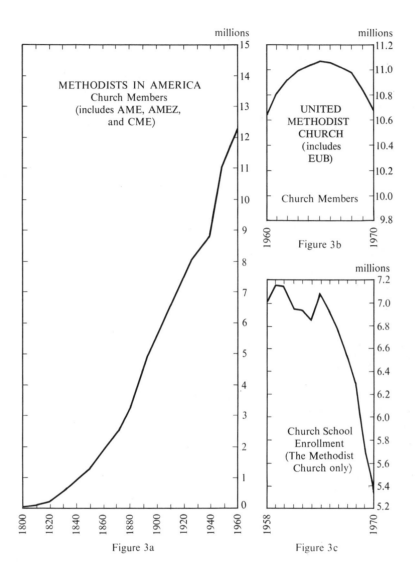

millions

METHODISTS IN AMERICA
Church Members
(includes AME, AMEZ,
and CME)

15
14
13
12
11
10
9
8
7
6
5
4
3
2
1
0

1800 1820 1840 1860 1880 1900 1920 1940 1960

Figure 3a

millions

UNITED
METHODIST
CHURCH
(includes
EUB)

Church Members

11.2
11.0
10.8
10.6
10.4
10.2
10.0
9.8

1960   1970

Figure 3b

millions

Church School
Enrollment
(The Methodist
Church only)

7.2
7.0
6.8
6.6
6.4
6.2
6.0
5.8
5.6
5.4
5.2

1958   1970

Figure 3c

graph for 1960–70 shows a composite statistic: the Methodist
Church (which accounts for the great bulk of Methodists: around
ten million in the decade shown) plus the Evangelical United
Brethren Church (a body of less than a million members), which
merged in 1968. This curve reached its peak in 1965 and then
began to decline, a process adumbrated by church school enrollment several years earlier.

Figures 4a, 4b, and 4c report Presbyterian membership.
Gaustad's graph (Fig. 4a) includes the main Presbyterian bodies,
north and south, while the enlarged graph for 1960–70 shows only
the largest body, the United Presbyterian Church in the USA,
which increased slowly between 1961 and 1965 and then began to
diminish, more and more precipitately. Its church school enrollment, shown in Fig. 4c, dropped off sooner and more sharply.

Figures 5a, 5b, and 5c show the membership of the group
Gaustad calls Congregational, though the Congregational churches
merged with the Christian Church in 1931 and with the Evangelical
and Reformed Church (itself the product of a merger) in 1957. It
is the combined body, the United Church of Christ, that is reported
in the enlarged graphs for 1960–70. Reports for this denomination
are not available in the 1960 and 1961 *Yearbooks*, and the 1963
report appears anomalous. The 1962 figure, however, fits a line of
gradual increase culminating in 1964 and 1965, when a steep decline began. Church school enrollment figures for the decade show
nothing but decline, though not as steep as church membership.

These five sets of graphs portray the membership trends for
five major Protestant families, the main body of each being one
of the five "wheel-horses" of the ecumenical movement in the
United States, namely: the United Methodist Church, the Episcopal
Church, the United Presbyterian Church in the USA, the Lutheran
Church in America, and the United Church of Christ. All five
show a significant decline in the latter half of the decade, within a
year or two of each other. This may be merely a temporary lull
before a new advance, or it may be the beginning of a serious and
progressive deterioration.

(Trends in other bodies, including the Roman Catholic Church,

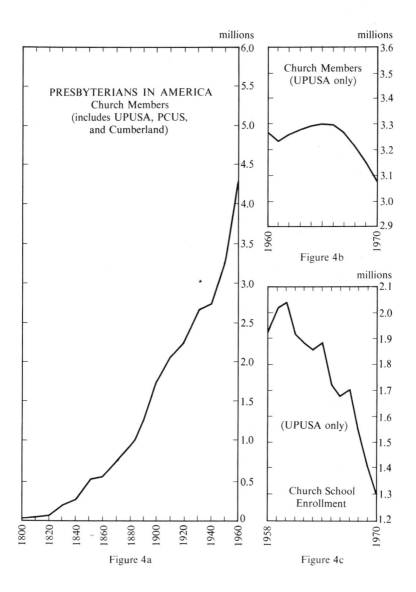

millions

PRESBYTERIANS IN AMERICA
Church Members
(includes UPUSA, PCUS,
and Cumberland)

Figure 4a

millions

Church Members
(UPUSA only)

Figure 4b

millions

(UPUSA only)

Church School
Enrollment

Figure 4c

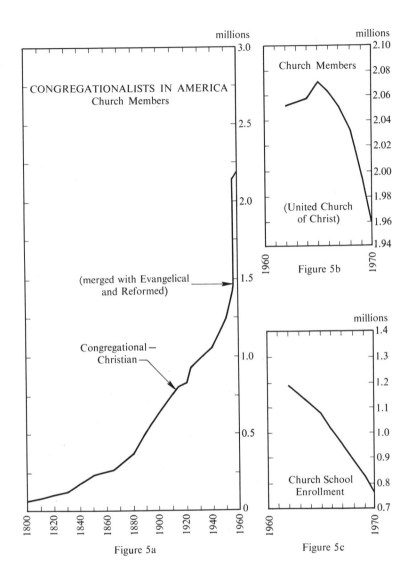

CONGREGATIONALISTS IN AMERICA
Church Members

(merged with Evangelical and Reformed)

Congregational — Christian

Figure 5a

Church Members

(United Church of Christ)

Figure 5b

Church School Enrollment

Figure 5c

will be noted in the next chapter. No statistical analysis of the Eastern Orthodox churches or of the predominantly black denominations has been attempted because their ethnic character suggests that the dynamics at work in them are significantly different from those that form the basis of this study.)

Other Signs of Decline

With decrease in membership has come decrease in contributions for many of these denominations, though some have shown an encouraging financial rally in 1970 despite continuing membership shrinkage. Sharp cutbacks in the budgets of denominational agencies and administrative headquarters have been necessary. The Episcopal Church, for instance, at the end of 1970 reduced the staff of its executive council from 203 to 104!

Many local congregations have felt similar influences in the past few years, particularly marginal parishes which were already struggling to survive. The aggregate number of local churches of the major denominations decreased during the 1960's. Church construction (including educational and other buildings) has decreased steadily for six years.

1965	$1,207,000,000
1966	1,164,000,000
1967	1,093,000,000
1968	1,038,000,000
1969	949,000,000
1970	921,000,000[2]

And now the market for church publications seems to be drying up. Many denominational periodicals have merged, reduced their frequency of publication, or discontinued altogether. Several church publishing houses have likewise consolidated, merged, closed, or been sold. This trend is partly the result of rising costs that have afflicted all publications. But it is noteworthy that some

2. U.S. Department of Commerce statistics, cited by Religious News Service, May 20, 1971.

trade publishers have been cutting back on books about churches. As one of them commented late in 1970, "We . . . have learned that at least in our market, which is basically the general bookstore, the interest in books concerned with the organized Church, especially books that do not sensationalize the problems, has waned to the point where there is basically none left."

In the past fourteen years, the number of missionaries sent abroad by six major Protestant denominations has diminished:[3]

Overseas task force	1958	1971
American Baptist Convention	407	290
United Presbyterian Church USA	1293	810
Presbyterian Church US	504	391
United Methodist Church (incl. EUB)	1453	1175
Episcopal Church	395	138
United Church of Christ	496	356
	4548	3160

In view of these developments, it is not surprising that in public-opinion polls more and more people are responding that religion is losing influence—whatever that may mean.

Proportion Saying Religion Is Losing Influence[4]

1957	14%
1962	31%
1965	45%
1967	57%
1968	67%

The churches may be experiencing the same secular miseries as have befallen Lockheed, the *Saturday Evening Post*, and the Penn Central. But a period of general financial hardship does not by itself bring down the giants. Rather, it provides a time of testing in which organizations can demonstrate whether they are vigorous and adaptable or rigid, inert, and ready to fall. Adverse seasons provide the occasion rather than the cause of decline.

3. "The Missionary Retreat," *Christianity Today,* Nov. 19, 1971, pp. 26, 27.
4. Gallup Report, May 25, 1968.

To be sure, there are also encouraging developments among the churches, such as the increase in some seminary enrollments. And some of the negative developments may be consequences of over-expansion, or the result of secular trends such as urbanization, or actually blessings in disguise. But there is sufficient basis in fact to ask: *What's happened to the churches?*

Proposed Remedies

Rare is the local church in these latter days whose elders are not called together in some current crisis of survival for a session of institutional soul-searching on this problem. A composite account of their deliberations might read as follows.

CHAIRMAN: We can't go on like this. We've got a deficit of $_____, and the winter fuel bill will be due at the end of this month and there's the repair of the drainpipes that's got to be done as soon as it warms up a little, and the organ needs tuning, and . . .

TREASURER: The collections are down a third from what they were this time last year.

CHOIR DIRECTOR: It's because people aren't coming to church on Sunday morning. Our attendance isn't half what it used to be!

CHURCH SCHOOL SUPT.: We've lost three teachers in the past month —though we've got more than enough left to take care of the number of children that still come: only we'll have to combine several age groups . . .

TRUSTEE: It's getting to be too big a load for the membership. Why don't we see if the congregation at St. James would be interested in merging? We could sell one of the buildings and both meet in the other one.

PRESIDENT OF LADIES' AUXILIARY: Well, I wouldn't want to sell *this* one. My grandfather helped build it.

STEWARD: St. James won't want to sell, either. My brother-in-law goes there, and they're really devoted to their church.

CHAIRMAN: Then what *are* we going to do?

PRESIDENT OF MEN'S CLUB: What we need is something to give people more interest in the church, so they'll feel they're getting something out of it.

DEACON: That's right! What we need are more social affairs.

TREASURER: We could have another clambake; we made two hundred dollars on the last one.

DEACON: I don't mean just money-raisers, but things people could come out to for the fellowship.

PRESIDENT OF YOUTH GROUP: And the entertainment. Why couldn't we show movies on Saturday evenings, or hold a dance, or . . . ?

PRESIDENT OF LADIES' AUXILIARY: That would be all right for the young people, but the adults wouldn't come out for movies or a dance.

PRESIDENT OF MOTHERS' CLUB: Couples with young children have a hard time getting out to evening affairs, they have to get a baby-sitter . . .

CHOIR DIRECTOR: Why couldn't the youth group provide free baby-sitter service?

PRESIDENT OF YOUTH GROUP: Because we want to go to the dance ourselves!

CHAIRMAN: Perhaps if we send out a letter to all the members explaining our difficulties, they might increase their contributions.

PRESIDENT OF MEN'S CLUB: We don't want to drive them away. Nobody likes to be part of an organization that's got troubles. And they don't like to be hit for more money either, unless they can see what they're going to get for it.

PRESIDENT OF LADIES' AUXILIARY (*dubiously*): I suppose the women could put on another rummage sale . . .

CHOIR DIRECTOR: If we could just get people out on Sunday morning like we used to, that'd go a long way toward solving the problem. I should think the pastor would get discouraged preaching to so few people!

CHURCH SCHOOL SUPT.: We could divide the congregation up into teams and give prizes for the team that gets the most people out to church.

PRESIDENT OF MOTHERS' CLUB: We've *done* all those things before, and none of them helped. We don't need more sales, more social events, more entertainments. People can get those somewhere else if they want them. They come to church for *religion,* and if they don't get it, why should they come for anything else? Maybe we ought to ask whether we're giving people the *religious* help they need. (*Brief silence. Then—*)

CHAIRMAN: How about each member of the board promising to attend church every Sunday and bring another family with him?

PRESIDENT OF MEN'S CLUB: Not during the summer. I couldn't promise for then because of vacations . . . (*And so on into the night.*)

The foregoing dialogue is not imaginary. I heard it recently at a little crossroads church in suburbia. It is almost identical with similar discussions heard in each of five local churches I served as pastor. The only unusual feature was the comment about religion. No one answered the young mother. The pastor was not present, being a seminary student away at school during the week; she might not have said what she did if he had been there.

Apart from the small silence after her suggestion, the discussion went on as though she had not spoken. No argument, no agreement, no response at all. Those present did not know quite what to do with that kind of comment. It did not fit into their sphere of discourse at all, particularly not at a serious church board meeting. Yet in a few words she summed up the thesis of this book and supplied the final provocation for putting it down on paper.

Similar discussions take place at more exalted levels of the church. Learned theologians, ethicists, and denominational executives ask the same kinds of questions and give the same kinds of answers, though possibly with greater erudition.

Some contend that the churches are declining because they are simply not relevant to the needs of the day. To become more *relevant*, it seems, they should show a greater interest in social problems and engage in more vigorous programs of social action and welfare. Others argue that the sectarian divisions of the church impair its witness and hasten its decline. They urge a *broader ecumenism*, such as the proposed union of nine major denominations to form the "Church of Christ Uniting" or the proposed National Conference of Churches, which is designed to include the Roman Catholic Church and others not presently in the ecumenical mainstream. And many other remedies are urged upon the churches daily:

A more contemporary liturgy, making fuller use of the arts.

Better and more professional pastoral counseling.

A revival of great preaching.

New methods and media of evangelism.

Identification with the empowerment of oppressed minorities.

Greater empathy with the youth culture.

A return to the Bible.

Cultivation of gifts of the Spirit: speaking in tongues, prophecy, faith-healing, etc.

A stronger program of stewardship.

More time and resources for religious education.

The remedy may be any or all of these or none. It is difficult to select an appropriate remedy until the ailment has been identified and understood, which is the purpose of the present book.

Church Membership Statistics

Some readers may wonder if we are not making too much of a few membership statistics. Church statistics are notoriously unreliable, some feel. And many churches would be better off with fewer members, so why draw negative attention to those that may be simply trying to eliminate dead wood from overinflated rolls? This uneasiness boils down to several significant but separable points.

1. "Church membership statistics are *inflated*." True. No church admits to membership losses if it can help it, and every church minimizes those it does admit. This provides, if anything, a conservative bias for my hypothesis: that is, if a church is losing members by its own admission, the shrinkage must be at least as great as is admitted.

2. "Church membership statistics are *unreliable*." This charge is truer of some churches than of others. Most of the major denominations are fairly conscientious and consistent about collecting and reporting their membership figures. Those that are not are readily recognizable by the figures themselves. Any time-series based on large-scale phenomena (such as membership in a body of several million members) will behave in a fairly stable manner, barring catastrophic events of pervasive effect or a shift in the basis of reporting. Any such series of numbers which fluctuates erratically over time without ascertainable cause cannot be relied on and is not used in this study. Those I have used show relative stability over a decade or more, suggesting that any errors,

vagaries, or reporting biases are constant, minimal, or compensating; and if constant, are in the direction adverse to our hypothesis (see No. 1 above)—i.e., the argument does not gain by them.

3. "Church membership statistics are *incommensurable*." That is, membership does not mean the same thing to Roman Catholics as it does to Mormons, for instance. Some Roman Catholic parishes count as members every baptized member of every family in the parish. Some other churches have a long and rigorous course of training for membership (as most Roman Catholic parishes have for converts). Churches also vary in the ease with which members may be expelled for misconduct or dropped for inactivity. But so long as standards for entering and leaving remain relatively constant within a given church, the time-series of its aggregate membership is comparable with that of another church. That is, we are not concerned with the relative magnitude of the churches but with the increase or decrease over time. Whatever membership means to a given church, is it getting more of it or less?

4. "Church membership statistics are not *valid*." That is, they do not measure what we are using them to measure: social strength. It is conceivable, we are reminded, that a church could tighten up its standards of membership, resulting in a loss of substandard members and a slower or reversed growth rate. That church would be stronger than one whose membership continued to expand with vast accessions of merely nominal adherents.

It is conceivable, to be sure, that one or more of the denominations I have characterized as declining is actually reducing its impedimenta and becoming stronger thereby. Conceivable—but not very likely. Such a body would become straightway an object of exceptional note in the religious world. Unfortunately, no such notable prodigies of self-denial have arisen in ecumenical circles lately.

In the Old Testament there is the tradition of a Saving Remnant —the handful of faithful who remain true to the covenant—the archetype of which is Gideon's army (Judg. 7:1-7), deliberately reduced to three hundred men of exceptional quality, a band as strong or stronger than the original throng. Perhaps something of the kind will happen—or could or should happen—in the churches today. But however desirable, this is not what is going on at present in the diminishing denominations. What we see in them is not a Saving Remnant but just an ordinary remnant of dwindling vitality.

Though membership statistics are not the only index of social strength, yet they do point to a certain inescapable, irreducible, quantifiable "thereness" in an organization, which has some direct and discernible relation to its existence and success. That is, organizations are made up of members. Whatever its optimum size, an organization that is losing this essential substance is in a distinctly different state from one that is gaining it. If a man is progressively losing weight, he and his family and friends begin to worry about his health. There may be many reasons for the loss— and it may indeed be a healthy one—but his physician will want to be quite sure he knows what is going on and that he has the process under control, since diminution can proceed only so far. Beyond that there is no patient left. The physician can usually determine by secondary symptoms whether the loss is healthy or not.

Likewise with organizations: consistent loss of substance is an important change which may have various explanations, but its causes need urgently to be known, lest it prove fatal. Whether such loss is healthy can often be determined by secondary characteristics, but even "healthy" decrease ceases to be so if carried too far. Even Gideon's band had to have three hundred members—he couldn't do it alone.

Chapter II

Is Religion Obsolete?

In seeking the cause of the deterioration of an organization—whether it be *Collier's*, Lockheed, or the Penn Central—there are at least two kinds of explanation, depending upon whether the fault lies with the organization or with the times. The latter class includes various forms of *obsolescence*: the product or service provided by the organization is no longer needed (e.g., buggy whips) or has been replaced by more modern equivalents (e.g., square-rigged sailing ships), or the production process has been superseded by more efficient methods (as in the manufacture of cigars, formerly handmade). The other class of explanation points to some sort of *internal failure*: the inability of the organization to provide a needed product or service for reasons of incompetence or inefficiency. If an outfit fails to modernize, to diversify, to develop new products, incompetence might be charged to it, but for our purposes at the moment it will be preferable to give the organization the benefit of the doubt and attribute the difficulty to the pace of change.

When we seek the cause of the deterioration of churches, then, we may consider under the heading of obsolescence any explanation that would locate the trouble not in the churches themselves but in the times, such as: (*a*) that religion is no longer needed, or (*b*) that churches are no longer needed, or (*c*) that the current output is hopelessly out-of-date. In this chapter we shall explore such exonerating explanations.

17

Religion Is No Longer Needed

Some people feel that religion has served its purpose—if it ever had one. "It may have been useful as a device for social control in the days before science and democracy and the industrial revolution, but now we've outgrown all that." Some would agree with Karl Marx that religion is the opium of the masses, clouding man's ability to perceive his problems, dulling his power to solve them rationally and scientifically.

For some of our most intelligent and cultivated contemporaries it is already excess baggage. They go about their various pursuits without reference to it. This is not necessarily a modern development. There have always been more people whose lives were not significantly affected by religion than religious leaders—or such people themselves—liked to admit. The new development is that today everyone admits it. There is no longer the obligation to *appear* to be religious or give lip-service to the importance and validity of religion, and many people just don't bother. If social status and acceptability no longer depend upon one's piety, why pretend to be pious?

Perhaps it is this emancipation from the social pressures toward hypocrisy that has undercut support for religion. There may still be members of an older generation who haven't yet got the message that religion is passé, but eventually they will die out and even the vestiges of religion will disappear—or so some predict.

No age is without its futurists, who appear ignorant of history and its evidence of the massive continuity and intractability of the human species. Even as the *philosophes* welcomed the Age of Reason and the enlightened Religion of Humanity, so today there are those who think that man is entering a new Age of Aquarius, an era of "Consciousness III" or McLu'nacy, some computerized utopia of leisure and affluence and togetherness. As the Old Era yields to the New, religion withers away (like the state?) and Modern Man goes forth into the radiant dawn of a New Day, unfettered by outmoded rites and obsolete beliefs.

Churches Are No Longer Needed

Others are less sweeping in their diagnosis. They may concede that some kind of religion will linger on, but insist it will do so without the ecclesiastical encumbrances which they view as the real burden on man's spirit. In every age and culture priesthood and temple have earned much obloquy, but in our day of growing disenchantment with vast bureaucratic organizations, they are apt to receive even more than their deserved share of criticism.

Some such critics will be content to view the difficulties of the churches as resulting from defects, deterioration, or overextension in a type of organization which is no better and no worse than others. But there will be some who see these things as a fitting judgment on a social structure that is obtrusively unnecessary, exploiting man's gullibility and submissiveness for its own profit.

Current Output Is Out-of-Date

A third group could accept the existence of religion and even endure the survival of churches, if religious beliefs were not so absurd and churchly requirements so unreasonable. Sectarian differences were considered tiresome a century ago—how much more so today! If the various religious groups can't get together, how can they expect anyone to take them seriously?

With the advance of science, we are told, belief in the super-natural—magic, miracles, divine beings, heaven and hell—long ago became untenable. Religion has been retreating ever since, but apparently not fast enough. The remaining absurdities have crumbled, leaving the churches with little to offer. Men are no longer interested in God-language, some say. For modern man, "God is dead."

The death of God does not necessarily mean the death of religion, we are assured. A more reasonable religious enterprise might continue, if only it did not insist on belief in unprovable dogmas and would emphasize ethical principles which can be demonstrated from man's daily experience. It should not require conformity to rigid and arbitrary standards, such as abstaining from certain foods or beverages, or prescribing certain modes of sexual behavior and proscribing others. Furthermore, it should display a commitment to the solving of current social problems. And there must be no drawing of invidious distinctions between the saved and the damned, between saints and sinners.

For such a tolerant, reasonable, and relevant religion modern man might perhaps be able to find a place in his brave new world. He might even admit a sufficiently chastened, nonexclusive, and uncensorious church.

Thus we have noted three assessments of obsolescence in the churches: (1) modern man no longer needs religion; or (2) even if he wants religion, he no longer needs churches; or (3) even if he wants religion and churches, he doesn't want those with (*a*) absurd beliefs, (*b*) unreasonable requirements, (*c*) irrelevant preoccupations, or (*d*) invidious distinctions between those who belong and those who don't.

These are rather commonly accepted assessments among many sophisticated people today, though seldom explicitly stated because they are no longer daring enough to be interesting. In fact, the only noteworthy feature about these three axioms of the prevailing wisdom is that *they are directly contrary to the evidence*.

But Some Churches Are Growing!

Those who plead obsolescence as an explanation for organizational deterioration must rely rather heavily upon a similar state of affairs afflicting other structures similarly engaged. It is awkward indeed if the competition is thriving, growing, proliferating in what is supposed to be a uniformly hostile climate. Such a state of affairs casts doubt upon the whole notion that the trouble is in the times and not in the particular organization. Yet this is precisely the situation among the churches: *not all religious bodies are declining*. While most of the mainline Protestant denominations are trying to survive what they hope will be but a temporary adversity, other denominations are overflowing with vitality, such as the Southern Baptist Convention, the Assemblies of God, the Churches of God, the Pentecostal and Holiness groups, the Evangelicals, the Mormons (Church of Jesus Christ of Latter-Day Saints), Jehovah's Witnesses, Seventh-day Adventists, Black Muslims, and many smaller groups hardly even visible to the large denominations. Their statistics show a startling contrast to those in the preceding chapter.

Figure 6 shows a comparison of growth rates between two long-time rivals, the Southern Baptist Convention and the Methodist Church. In 1967, the former overtook the latter and has continued to increase at a rate of 2.26% per year, while the latter has begun to diminish, despite its merger with the Evangelical United Brethren Church in 1968. But even with the addition of 737,000 former EUB members, the United Methodist Church is not as large as the Southern Baptist Convention, which (unlike the United Methodist Church) is still increasing.

The foreign missionary personnel of the Southern Baptist Convention more than doubled, from 1,186 in 1958 to 2,494 in 1971, while the United Methodist overseas task force decreased from 1,453 to 1,175 in the same period.[1]

Figure 7 is a reminder of the membership trends of the other large Protestant denominations mentioned in the preceding chapter. The three Lutheran churches are shown separately. It is evident that of the six shown only the Lutheran Church–Missouri Synod is still increasing, and this at a decreasing rate, no longer matching the rate of U.S. population increase.

Figure 8 includes the membership rates for five rapidly growing churches of 250,000-400,000 members: the Seventh-day Adventists (3.2% increase per year), the Church of the Nazarene (2.6% increase), the Jehovah's Witnesses (5% increase per year), the Salvation Army (average 2.9% increase per year) and the Chris-

1. "The Missionary Retreat," *Christianity Today,* Nov. 19, 1971, pp. 26, 27.

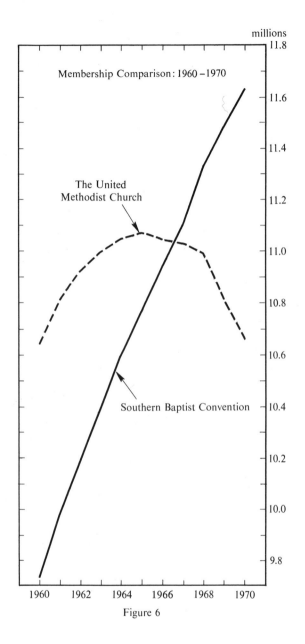

millions

Membership Comparison: 1960 –1970

The United
Methodist Church

Southern Baptist Convention

Figure 6

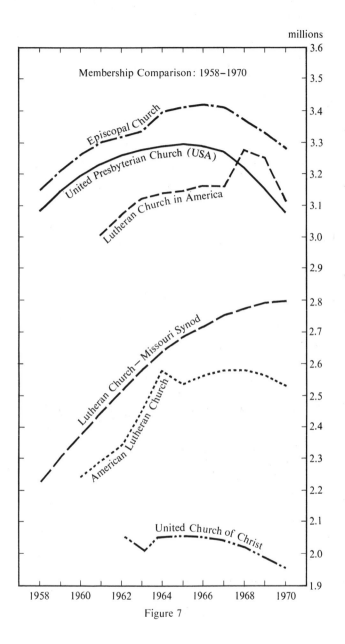

millions

Membership Comparison: 1958–1970

Episcopal Church

United Presbyterian Church (USA)

Lutheran Church in America

Lutheran Church—Missouri Synod

American Lutheran Church

United Church of Christ

1958 1960 1962 1964 1966 1968 1970

Figure 7

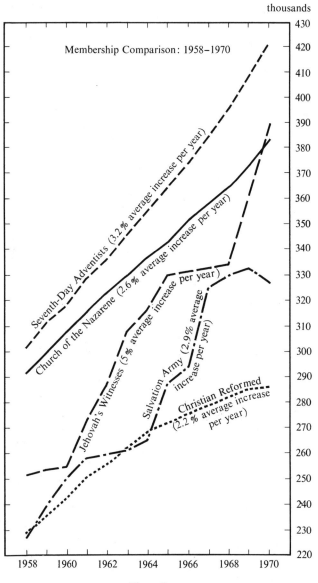

thousands

Membership Comparison: 1958–1970

Seventh-Day Adventists (3.2% average increase per year)

Church of the Nazarene (2.6% average increase per year)

Jehovah's Witnesses (5% average increase per year)

Salvation Army (2.9% average increase per year)

Christian Reformed (2.2% average increase per year)

Figure 8

tian Reformed Church (2.2% per year). They are designated as rapidly growing because their growth rates exceed the rate of population growth.

Others in this category (not shown because of scale differences) are: Free Methodist Church (1.6% increase—from 54,942 in 1958 to 64,394 in 1969); Assemblies of God (2.1% increase— from 505,552 in 1958 to 625,027 in 1969); Pentecostal Holiness Church (3.9% increase—from 49,594 in 1958 to 66,790 in 1969); and Church of Jesus Christ of Latter-day Saints (Mormons, Salt Lake City, Utah: 5.6% increase—from 1,394,729 in 1958 to 2,180,064 in 1968). No figures are available for the Churches of Christ, the Black Muslims, the Church of Christ, Scientist, and some others which may also be increasing rapidly. The rapidly growing bodies have also been increasing their missionary outreach while the mainline denominations have been cutting back. In 1958, the Evangelical Foreign Missions Association had 4,688 missionaries abroad and by 1971 this number had increased to 7,479, an increase of about 60%. The Wycliffe Bible Translators, beginning in 1935, reached 705 staff members abroad by 1958 and grew to 1762 in 1970! Dr. David Stowe, head of the United Church of Christ Board for World Ministries, observed that "the fundamentalists and pentecostals increased their numbers at about the same rate as the mainline churches' decrease."[2] By this important index of spiritual vitality, the mainline churches are weakening while the rapidly growing churches are becoming stronger.

They Are the "Wrong" Churches!

These groups not only give evidence that religion is not obsolete and churches not defunct, but they contradict the contemporary notion of an acceptable religion. They are not "reasonable," they are not "tolerant," they are not ecumenical, they are not "relevant." Quite the contrary!

2. *Ibid.*

They often refuse to recognize the validity of other churches' teachings, ordinations, sacraments. They observe unusual rituals and peculiar dietary customs, such as foot-washing and vegetarianism among Seventh-day Adventists, abstention from stimulants among Mormons. They disregard the "decent opinions of mankind" by persisting in irrational behavior, such as the Jehovah's Witnesses' refusal of blood transfusions. They try to impose uniformity of belief and practice among members by censorship, heresy trials, and the like. For instance, the Southern Baptist Convention recently ordered the Broadman Press—its publishing house—to withdraw a biblical commentary which the Convention deemed too liberal; the President of the Lutheran Church–Missouri Synod, J. A. O. Preuss, undertook a personal investigation of Concordia Seminary to discover any faculty members whose teaching was not compatible with the faith of the church; the Salvation Army (in England) has expelled Major Fred Brown for publishing religious writings without first clearing them with his superiors. Some of these various bodies display the highest incidence of anti-Semitism among major religious organizations (cf. Glock & Stark, *Christian Beliefs and Anti-Semitism*).[3]

It is ironic that the religious groups which persist in such "unreasonable" and "unsociable" behavior should be flourishing, while the more "reasonable" and "sociable" bodies are not. It is not only ironic, but it suggests that our understanding of what causes a religious group to flourish is inadequate. Some dynamic seems to be at work which contradicts prevailing expectations. Such a dynamic will be traced in the following chapters; a motive power which may also account for the peculiarities noted.

Another student of social dynamics, Professor George R. La-Noue, Jr. of Teacher's College, Columbia University, has independently reached similar conclusions by a comparison of paired religious groups. He matched liberal against conservative branches of several denominational families in the United States, as shown in the accompanying graphs (Figs. 9-14), using percent of annual membership increase (for years through 1968, computed from 1940 as the base year) rather than straight membership totals.

3. New York: Harper & Row, 1969.

He notes that the liberal branches seem more attuned to the social and demographic trends of the modern population. They are more urbanized and cosmopolitan. They enjoy greater affluence and mobility. Their members have more education on the average than do those of the conservative branches. One would expect them, therefore, to appeal more successfully to an increasingly urban, affluent, educated, and mobile population than could the conservative branches, and thus to attract more members and grow more rapidly.

But in every case in his study (made of years before the sharp decline), the conservative branches are increasing proportionately more rapidly than the liberal! He explains this anomaly by a theory which is similar in many ways to the one advanced in this volume, and it will be introduced for purposes of comparison at the appropriate place.

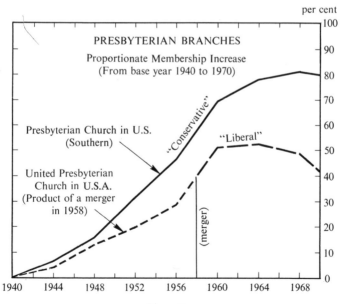

Figure 9

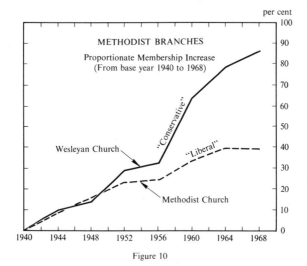

Figure 10

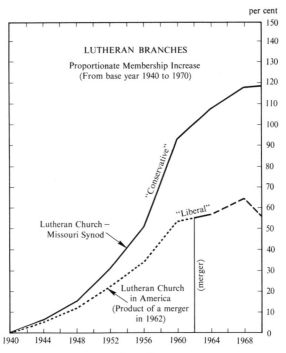

Figure 11

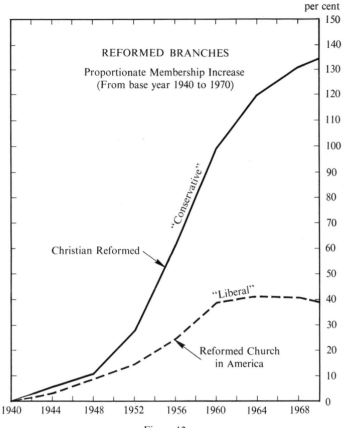

per cent

REFORMED BRANCHES

Proportionate Membership Increase
(From base year 1940 to 1970)

"Conservative"

Christian Reformed

"Liberal"

Reformed Church
in America

Figure 12

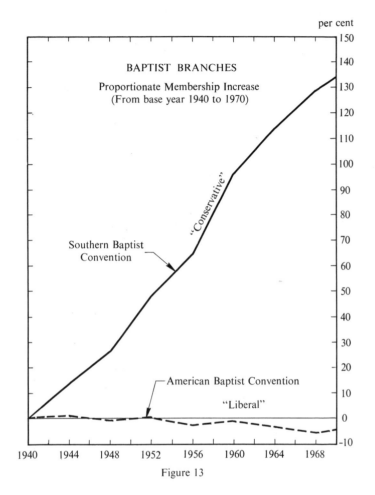

Figure 13

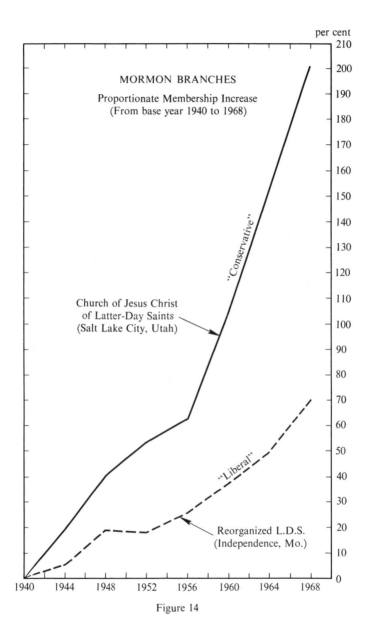

MORMON BRANCHES

Proportionate Membership Increase
(From base year 1940 to 1968)

per cent

"Conservative"

Church of Jesus Christ
of Latter-Day Saints
(Salt Lake City, Utah)

"Liberal"

Reorganized L.D.S.
(Independence, Mo.)

Figure 14

The Roman Catholic Church

In the contrast between "reasonable," tolerant, ecumenical, "relevant," liberal churches and "unreasonable," intolerant, non-ecumenical, "otherwordly," conservative churches there is a unique case deserving special attention: a church that has moved from the latter camp to the former in an incredibly short period of time— between five and ten years—a remarkable feat for the largest Christian body in the world: the Roman Catholic Church!

Before Vatican Council II, it was unyielding in its unwillingness to admit the existence of other Christian groups or to call them churches. It insisted upon such dietary and sumptuary rules as meatless Fridays, Saturday confession, distinctive garb for priests and nuns. No religious group has been more adamant in its doc-trinally-determined policies than has the Roman Catholic Church in regard to priestly celibacy, birth control, and abortion. It yielded to none in its determination to hunt out heresy and protect the faithful from scandal by censoring or prohibiting all unsuitable literature. And (until recently) a significant degree of anti-Semitism has been discernible even in the liturgy of the Church.

But all that is changed, or at least changing, since the windows were thrown open in the *aggiornamento* of Vatican II. The Church has begun to see some validity in other Christian (and even non-Christian) churches. It is groping toward a rapprochement on the problem of mixed marriages, in which the non-Catholic partner and his or her church may attain a greater degree of parity with the Catholic side. Fish on Friday is no longer obligatory. Individual confession may be replaced, in theory as it already is in fact, by collective confession or none. Some priests and nuns now wear secular clothes of their choosing and some religious orders are no longer cloistered away from the world. Large segments of the Church are resisting the authority of the Pope with respect to priestly celibacy, the pill, and even infallibility itself. The Index of Prohibited Books was ended several years ago, and no heresy prosecutions have been undertaken lately. The liturgy has not only been purged of its anti-Semitic references, but updated in other respects as well and rendered into the vernacular languages. It is a transformation such as few would have predicted a mere ten years ago.

What has been the result of this amazing effort to make the Roman Catholic Church more reasonable, more ecumenical, more acceptable, more tolerant, more relevant to today's world? Has it become stronger, more vigorous—vital—confident? Not exactly. It has suffered the defection of hundreds of priests and nuns, not to mention lay members.

A recent study[4] reported the following numbers of priests requesting release from clerical vows:

1963	167
1964	640
1965	1,128
1966	1,418
1967	1,769
1968	2,263
1969	2,963
1970	3,800
Total	14,148[5]

The Church has been confronted by varying forms and degrees of rebellion within the ranks, with nuns defying cardinals, priests demanding the removal of their bishops, and lay organizations publicly and persistently criticizing the hierarchy!

And in 1970 the Roman Catholic Church in the United States reported its first net loss of membership in this century (see Figs. 15a and 15b). Though a slight increase was reported the following

4. *Commonweal,* March 19, 1971, p. 26, reporting an article in *Diaspora,* newsletter of the Society of Priests for a Free Ministry, which cites a confidential report to the bishops by Pro Mundi Vita and research by François Houtart. Figures subsequently released by the Vatican are smaller, but show a similar increase in departures from the priesthood. The *Diaspora* account, however, estimates that at least as many more priests leave the church without formal permission, with highest losses (about 10%) occurring in the 30-45 age group.

5. Out of 540,000 priests in the Church, worldwide.

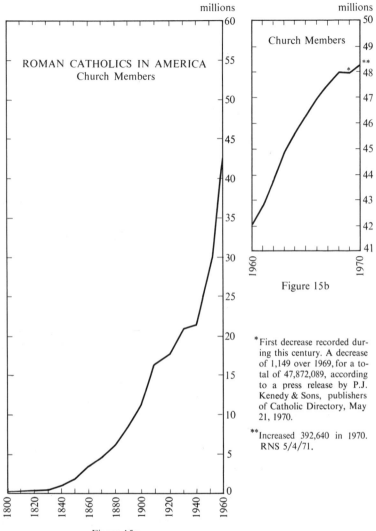

ROMAN CATHOLICS IN AMERICA
Church Members

Figure 15a

Church Members

Figure 15b

*First decrease recorded during this century. A decrease of 1,149 over 1969, for a total of 47,872,089, according to a press release by P.J. Kenedy & Sons, publishers of Catholic Directory, May 21, 1970.

**Increased 392,640 in 1970. RNS 5/4/71.

year, other indices continued to decline, suggesting that the once-unshakable church has fallen into serious disarray. It has "leaped over the wall" to join the liberal, "relevant," ecumenical churches —and is beginning to show the same symptoms. Why?

Some would say that they are all declining because they have not modernized rapidly enough; others consider it a regrettable but temporary trauma accompanying rapid change, which will subside when things settle down.

Is it possible that it is neither, but instead a direct *consequence* of modernization? Churches that have not tried to adjust to the times—to ingratiate themselves with the world—in many cases are not declining. In them we see no indication that religion is obsolete, churches outdated, or modernization helpful. They cause us to suspect that the declining churches are not victims of changing times but of internal failure—the inability to provide a needed product or service. They have not adequately understood or performed their essential business: the dispensing of religion. What is this business, and why does it matter whether it is performed?

Chapter III

The Indispensable Function of Religion

Not only are some religious groups still thriving, but new ones are constantly coming into being, some of them quite unconventional and even bizarre in character. At the very moment when it begins to be accepted that religion is no longer needed and churches are expiring, new manifestations of religiousness appear where least expected—among adolescents and young adults—the very age groups which had most visibly abandoned the conventional religious bodies in seeming apathy and disillusionment.

On college campuses and in sophisticated urban circles, devotees of Zen Buddhism, yoga, and other exotic Eastern religions spring up, competing for adherents with neoastrology, satanism, witchcraft, hallucinogenic cults, and various free-form mysticisms. Among the young men and women who have dropped out of college and the career rat-race the same searching for something remarkably similar to religion is seen. Communes develop semisacramental rituals for the sharing of their macrobiotic diet, and vagrant elements of everything from voodoo to Vedanta are celebrated in a growing preoccupation with the irrational, the mystic, the mysterious. Popular magazines have discovered this new (or very old) phenomenon and gilded it with notoriety as deceptive as its former obscurity. On the West Coast, hundreds of "street people" are reportedly being converted (back?) to Christianity by "Jesus freaks" preaching and praying in the parks and on the streetcorners and beaches of Seattle, Portland, San Francisco, Los Angeles.[1]

These developments do not prove that a return to religion is imminent or that "it's only a matter of time until men come back to the church." They merely remind us that man is an incorrigibly religious creature who wants to make sense out of his life—in unorthodox terms, if necessary, or even in orthodox ones. Religion is everywhere; man cannot manage long without it. As Talcott Parsons noted in his introduction to Max Weber's classic *Sociology of Religion:* " . . . there is no known human society without something which modern social scientists would classify as religion. . . . Religion is as much a human universal as language."[2]

This has led many to conclude that religion must serve some essential function for man. J. Milton Yinger remarks in *The Scientific Study of Religion*, "It is widely held by students of society that there are certain functional prerequisites without which society would not continue to exist. At first glance, this seems to be obvious—scarcely more than to say that an automobile engine could not exist, as a going system, without a carburetor. . . . Most writers list religion among the functional prerequisites."[3] What function is religion performing that is as essential to mankind as a carburetor is to an automobile? There are almost as many answers to this question as there are sociologists of religion, but most of their answers can be subsumed under a broad heading of which they are each special cases. What religion is "doing" in every instance (albeit with greater or lesser effectiveness) is *explaining the meaning of life in ultimate terms.*

One religion may bring its adherents to submit to social control or to be content with their lot in life by the way it explains man's nature and destiny. Another, perhaps within the same society, may arouse its followers to rebellion against the same conditions by in-

---

1. See cover article "The New Rebel Cry: Jesus Is Coming!" in *Time,* June 21, 1971; also news columns in *Christianity Today,* January 29, 1971, pp. 34-35; also Sara Davidson's account "The Rush for Instant Salvation," *Harper's Magazine,* July, 1971.

2. Boston: Beacon Press, 1963, pp. xxvii, xxviii.

3. New York: Macmillan Co., 1970, p. 21.

terpreting what life is all about, but in a different way. Both are fulfilling the same essential function for their members and thereby for society as a whole. One faith may help to integrate society by preaching brotherly love to its members; another may contribute to its disintegration by preaching a holy war against other factions. Yet both are explaining life to their respective adherents.

In each instance religion is doing the same thing, whether the incidental historical outcome be passivity or rebellion, integration or disruption. It is "making sense" out of existence. There is no necessity that it be the same sense for all. But then why is the performance of this function so important? Why is it a universal "functional prerequisite" of human societies? What happens if it isn't done?

The Business of Religion Is Meaning

Man is an inveterate meaning-monger. He tries to make sense out of his experience, even if he has to resort to non-sense to do it. His eye involuntarily finds patterns in any random visual stimuli presented to it, and thus the night sky becomes peopled with constellations. His mind finds patterns in his experience, and accordingly the universe has become peopled with shapes and rhythms, powers and beings, fates and forces which enable him to make sense of it.

Some of these patterns are useful for managing the mundane affairs of life. ("Red sky at morning, sailors take warning.") Others suggest what may be expected of one's fellow men. ("Never trust a stranger." "Blood is thicker than water." "Beware of Greeks bearing gifts." "There's a sucker born every minute.") But by far the most important patterns for man's life are the very biggest ones, which explain the purpose of his existence, the nature of reality, the fate of the world, the character of the beings or forces that determine his destiny, and how he can relate to them. These largest patterns of meaning are the subject matter of religion.

These meanings may be couched in myths, legends, proverbs,

adages, songs, parables, laws, creeds, rituals, letters, visions, "histories," or exhortations. They may or may not be true in the sense of empirical correspondence to objective data or of coherence with other public, generally shared knowledge; but they are profoundly true in the sense of producing important consequences in human life, of shaping the outlook and expectations of millions of men and their estimate of, and relations to, one another. In this sense, man's meanings have helped him to deal with some of life's most profound and least manageable problems.

Why are these greater meanings so important to him? Could he not get along without such esoteric speculations? Perhaps he could if he were not in the most essential sense—at the very core of his self-awareness and his perception of the world—a *meaning-oriented being*. But he seems to need them to answer a couple of ancient and persistent questions. The oldest question in human awareness is probably "How can I survive?" Religion is not of much direct help in dealing with it, for the answers to this question are essentially technological: things man can do directly with his hands to affect his environment, to wrest his livelihood from it and defend himself from its various harms, as by hunting, farming, fighting, cooperating, making and using language and tools, and so forth.

It is after this question has been answered (technologically) that the second-oldest question arises. When a man's son dies, or his eyesight fails, or his people are enslaved, he asks himself as Job did: "Why do bad things happen to me?" (Or in more generalized fashion: "Why do bad things happen to *us?*" or "Why do bad things happen?") The attempt to answer that question, in whatever form, is the beginning of religion, and it is essentially an other-than-technological pursuit. When man can *manage* the bad things and prevent them from happening, they no longer pose *religious* problems for him.[4]

The failure to answer the second-oldest question may prevent a man from surmounting the injuries and sufferings that befall

4. The distinction between technological and metatechnological activity, with only the latter being truly religious, is made by William Henry Bernhardt in *A Functional Philosophy of Religion* (Denver: Criterion Press, 1968).

him. He may become embittered and despairing, then listless and parasitic, or erratic, violent, "criminal"—even suicidal. (Émile Durkheim, in his classic study of suicide, identified this syndrome with the largest category of suicides, which he contended were caused by *anomie* (anomy) or "normlessness": in our terms a malady of the absence of meaning.) Why should a man work patiently, day after day, if things are going to turn out so badly for him? Why not just quit? Or why not take his neighbor's goods? Which brings him face to face with the third-oldest question: "If bad things happen to me, why shouldn't I pass them on to others?" And the answers to this query, as to the one before it, have to do with the nature and duty of man, the purpose of his existence, and other profound and all-encompassing issues.

Milton Yinger describes the subject matter of religion in this way:

> Paul Tillich has said that religion is that which concerns us ultimately. Robert Bellah has expressed the same idea: " . . . religion is a set of symbolic forms and acts which relate man to the ultimate condition of his existence." Though there are important disagreements concerning the ultimate problems for man, a great many people would accept the following as among the fundamental concerns of human societies and individuals: How shall we respond to the fact of death? Does life have some central meaning despite the suffering and the succession of frustrations and tragedies it brings with it? . . . How can we bring our capacity for hostility and our egocentricity sufficiently under control to allow the groups within which we live—without which our life would be impossible—to be kept together?
>
> . . . . Religion may develop an intellectual system to interpret and deal with these questions, but they must be seen first of all not as a group of rationally conceived problems, but as expressions of an underlying emotional need.
>
> Religion, then, can be defined as a system of beliefs and practices by means of which a group of people struggles with these ultimate problems of human life. . . .
>
> Although the ways of struggling with these ultimate problems are enormously diverse, and seem destined for continuous change, the problems themselves are universal. A society that did not furnish its

members with beliefs and practices that gave them a means of dealing with these ultimate problems would have to struggle along with an enormous burden of tragedy unallayed and hostility unrestrained—if indeed it could survive at all.[5]

Religious meanings are described as ultimate meanings for several reasons: they refer to the last, most inclusive or most valued things; they come at the end of a succession of questions about the *why* of human existence; and they are not proximate to, instrumental for, or derivative from other concerns.

Building a Sacred World

Peter Berger has developed the same subject in his remarkable book, *The Sacred Canopy*.[6] In more learned language and with all the appropriate scholarly apparatus, his first two chapters provide a solid theoretical framework for the function of religion which is very similar to that outlined in this chapter, though he approaches it in a different way. He characterizes every human society as "an enterprise of world-building," in the sense that man is not instinctually programed as the lower animals are. "Man must *make* a world for himself . . . he must construct a *human* world. This world, of course, is culture. . . . While it is necessary that such worlds be built, it is quite difficult to keep them going" (pp. 5, 6).

The human world of culture is kept going by the transmission of its humanly constructed and collectively shared meanings from each generation to the next. Each individual, in order to become a member of his culture, must acquire by socialization the main meanings of that culture. A culture which cannot hand on its world of shared meanings through time will not survive. One of the essential things a culture does for its members is to provide for them this socially constructed mental universe, this meaningful ordering of experience, which Berger terms a *nomos*, by which "the individual can 'make

5. Yinger, *op. cit.*, pp. 6-8, *passim.*
6. New York: Doubleday Anchor Books, 1967.

sense' of his own biography" (p. 21). An individual who cannot appropriate, internalize this culturally transmitted world of meaning, this nomos, is faced with meaninglessness or anomy, a dreaded "separation from the social world."

> The socially established nomos may thus be understood . . . as a shield against terror. . . .
>
> The ultimate danger . . . is the danger of meaninglessness. . . . To be in society is to be "sane" precisely in the sense of being shielded from the ultimate "insanity" of such anomic terror. Anomy is unbearable to the point where the individual may seek death in preference to it. Conversely, existence within a nomic world may be sought at the cost of life itself, if the individual believes that this ultimate sacrifice has nomic significance. . . .
>
> Every nomos is an area of meaning carved out of a vast mass of meaninglessness, a small clearing of lucidity in a formless, dark, always ominous jungle. [Pp. 22, 23]

This nomos is threatened by the marginal situations man faces, which place him on the edge of a little clearing of meaning and order staring out into the darkness of meaninglessness and chaos. Foremost among such marginal situations is death, which "threatens the basic assumptions of order on which society rests" (p. 23).

The socially established nomos attains its greatest solidity and reality when it is taken for granted. Whenever it attains this quality, "there occurs a merging of its meanings with what are considered to be the fundamental meanings in the universe. Nomos and cosmos appear to be coextensive" (p. 24). In Berger's thought, "cosmos" is the system of fundamental meanings believed to underlie and organize the universe. *"Religion is the human enterprise by which a sacred cosmos is established"* (p. 25—emphasis added). "By sacred is meant here a quality of mysterious and awesome power, other than man and yet related to him. . . ." (p. 25). It is the sacred cosmos that "provides man's ultimate shield against the terror of anomy" (p. 26), a sacred canopy against chaos. "A cosmos, as the ultimate ground and validation of human nomoi, need not necessarily be sacred. . . . [though] most of man's worlds have been sacred worlds. . . . Religion has played a strategic part in the human enterprise of world-building. . . . [It] is the audacious attempt to conceive of the entire universe as being humanly significant" (pp. 27-28).

The Difference Meaning Makes

If a man can see his sufferings—the bad things that befall him and those he loves—as part of a cosmic purpose or a long-range good, he can often overcome them, or at least regain some of his zest and resilience and possibly go on to significant achievements. Meaning—of a certain quality and in certain circumstances, to be described below—has historically and repeatedly proven to be the remedy for severe disorganization of persons and groups. It has been the antidote for anomy, the rehabilitator of criminals, the rescuer of alcoholics, the deliverer of drug addicts, the preventer of suicide, the cure for various psychosomatic disabilities, and the solution for many cases of poverty, failure, and despair. To be sure, not all such ailments yield to a given application of meaning; quite the contrary. Just as there are many medicines, so there are many forms and carriers of meaning, not all equally congenial to a particular patient.

Only the largest-scale meanings seem suitable to produce such results: those offered and validated by religion. They may indeed seem speculative, if not totally preposterous, to some, but this has not in the least inhibited their ability to transform men and groups into vigorous, dynamic, conquering movements, overcoming individual disabilities and discouragements, instilling new and rigorous standards of behavior in thousands of willing adherents. Even in dilute or thirdhand form, such meanings still lend significance and coherence to the lives of their descendants.

Every society needs a system of meaning (or several) to explain to its members why bad things happen. Not all will find the same explanations satisfying; some will not be satisfied by any. But as long as most of them find that life makes sense most of the time, the society can survive. If more and more of its citizens are unwilling to persist in their labors, turning instead to unproductive or even destructive activities, including crime and addiction, that society is in trouble. The trouble is essentially a *malady of meaning,* for which *the remedy is religious,* though not in the pietistic sense often advocated.

No Disembodied Meaning

If it is conceded, for the sake of argument, that the function of religion as here defined is indispensable to man, does it follow that churches are dispensable? How is the system of meaning—any system—to be transmitted from one generation to another without an organizational carrier of some kind? Neither anthropology nor history records a disembodied religion without any continuing group of people collectively experiencing and transmitting it. That group may not be called a church, it may not have an ordained clergy in the sense of full-time professionals set apart to specialize in religion. But there will be an organization of some kind, for without organization and institutionalization—a structure of roles and expectations handed on from generation to generation—any cultural pattern dies out.

More important, the meanings which religion provides gain their validity from a continuing group experience: they do not stand alone, in the abstract, nor above human prehension. Religious meaning doesn't "take" unless it is transmitted from one person to another, vouchsafed by the commitment of the bearer. From this point of view, there is no such thing as individual or instant or disembodied religion.

As Milton Yinger, querying, points out: "Can there be an 'individual' religion? There can be religious *aspects* of private systems of belief and action. A complete religion, however, is a social phenomenon: it is shared, and it takes on many of its most significant aspects only in the interaction of the group."[7] A religion doesn't become *visible* as such until it is shared by a committed

7. Yinger, *op. cit.,* p. 10.

group of people and has lasted at least a couple of generations. Until then, it is not so much a religion as a proposal for one. Whether the proposal is accepted by anyone remains to be seen.

If it is going to make the grade as a religion, it will have to become part of a stream of shared experience in which it meets the tests of various crises, doldrums, transitions, tensions, and attritions. That "stream of shared experience" in a "continuing community of adherents" is the religious organization—not only the carrier of the religion but its embodiment and validation. We could call it a church, except that not all churches are effective in fulfilling the religious function, and some groups which do fulfill it are not called churches.

Western societies used to insist that all citizens belong to the same church and believe the same meanings, but that arrangement often caused more problems than it solved. Modern societies are aware that men's interests in meanings differ, as do their tastes in literature, and that a variety of religions will satisfy the variety of citizens better than any one can do.[8]

Whatever undertakings make life meaningful in ultimate terms for their members, those enterprises are serving the religious function, irrespective of their ideology or structure, whether they claim to be doing so or not. (Despite its professed atheism, Marxism may serve this function for some.) When a religion is explaining life effectively for its members, it is serving the same function, to that extent, for the whole society—even for those citizens who are not aware of it. Another religion may perform this function for *them*. If a religion should set out deliberately to benefit the whole society by patriotic preaching or welfare services or social action, but *did not make life meaningful for its members*, it would benefit the whole society less than if it had contented itself with ministering its unique function to those who looked to it for that ministry.

This suggests a different measure of success among religious groups. Those are successful which are explaining life to their members so that it makes sense to them. They are successful— in a functional sense—whether they are viewed by outsiders as

8. Cf. William James, *The Varieties of Religious Experience.*

patriotic or unpatriotic, as pious or blasphemous, as quietist or activist, as pacifist or militant, as ecumenical or separatist, as liberal or conservative, as integrative or disruptive, as orthodox or heretical, or according to any of the many epithets applied to religions by outsiders. None of these adjectives tells us much about their effectiveness as religion, which is what really ought to matter to outsiders. Let us consider what kinds of measures will tell us something.

Chapter IV

Meaning, Demand, and Commitment

Man is a being who responds to *meaning*, perhaps in more ways, and more profound ways, than we have yet appreciated. It should not be surprising that this can be the key that unlocks some of his most intractable problems, such as anomie, addiction, and criminality. Perhaps, in working with human problems, we should not give up so quickly on the use of meaning to find a truly humane solution. Its use, however, cannot be just superficial moralizing or jawboning whereby those who do not directly face a problem try to preach a solution to those who do.

If meaning is the distinctively human ingredient in man's affairs, we might clarify our understanding if we viewed them from a more meaning-oriented standpoint. That is, what are the evidences of the emergence of meaning, its promulgation, its appropriation by few or many, its consequences in human life? To what degree has it evoked men's loyalties and their exertions? What are the dynamics of the contagion of meaning, its conflicts with other meanings, its utilization of power and utilization by power, its deterioration and evaporation?

History written from this viewpoint would not be just a recital of battles, treaties, and dynasties nor (in more recent vein) a catalog of industries, exports, and tariffs. Rather it would ask what meanings brought men into battle or built an economic system. This kind of history would not be just another dry exploit in the development of ideas—though the content of important meanings is certainly often connected with their effects, though not

always in the ways intended nor to the degree that historians of
ideas suppose.

Power—either military or economic—has been assumed to be
the main determinant of history, but *power depends upon the
ability to mobilize men around meaning.* Historians have begun to
recognize its role in generating the crusades and other wars of
religion (alas!) and in calling forth the development of science
and the industrial revolution.[1] Styles of history-writing swing from
greater to lesser emphasis on it: the American Civil War is seen
by some as a great crusade for the abolition of slavery, by others
as an effort of the agrarian South to free itself from northern industrial and financial overlordship. Obviously it was both, and some
other things as well. But the rallying of thousands of men around
the flags of abolition, of preserving the Union, or of defending the
"peculiar institution"—or their refusal to rally, as in the draft riots
in New York City—these meaning-tropic behaviors tell us more
about the distinctively human element in man's affairs than does
the fact that they fight over territory, dominance, or food, as non-
ideological animals do.

Some may insist that the banners of meaning around which men
rally are only rationalizations to justify their baser motives, but
the fact that such banners are useful, even necessary, to mobilize
men to great sacrifice and exertion is remarkable in itself. Men
will fight more intensely for abstract loyalties than they will for
booty. They will endure risk and deprivation longer for what they
believe in than they will for high wages under insignia in which they
do not believe.

We have seen the deterioration of American military forces in
Vietnam precisely as a result of the failure of meaning in that
enterprise. It just did not make sense to more and more of the
men who were expected to take risks, suffer, and die for it. Rather
than winning the hearts and minds of the people of Vietnam—an
enterprise in the realm of meaning—we were losing the hearts and
minds of Americans (both in Vietnam and in the United States)—

1. See the arguments over the role of Calvinism in shaping modern capitalism in Max Weber, *The Protestant Ethic and the Spirit of Capitalism,* and
R. H. Tawney, *Religion and the Rise of Capitalism,* etc.

likewise a transaction in the realm of meaning. The increase of drug addiction among U.S. military forces in Vietnam may be a symptom of growing boredom and alienation—which are meaning-maladies. The vast technological might of a great nation can destroy, but it cannot conquer, a tiny underdeveloped country when the latter has the morale, esprit, and determination that derive from shared meaning, while the former does not.

The Fullest Mobilization

No one knows what the full capacity of the human person is, especially for sustained, devoted, imaginative effort; it may never have been fully plumbed, let alone measured. But it is not likely that many of us are in danger of pressing the limits of human exertion or endurance. Physiologists tell us that normally only a small proportion of our physical and cerebral potential is utilized—how much less the more complex and exhausting creative and social proclivities of which we like to boast?

Suppose, to be charitable, that we are percolating along at about 20% of capacity most of the time. Sometimes, under the spur of ambition or stress, we may throw ourselves into a task with considerable energy and use as much as 40% for a little while. For the peripheral interests of our lives, which is what religion is for most people, we rarely expend more than a marginal 5% or 10% of our energy. And we never really get caught up fully and without reserve into anything above the 50% mark, if we can help it.

And all our lives we long to ease off from this arduous toil, this desperate exertion. We yearn to throttle down the old plant and lean back and take it easy—as though we ever took it hard. But on the rare occasions when we do relax more fully, we soon become restless and irritable. The vacationer may find himself after a while itching to get back to something "significant." The retired person may feel his long-awaited rest becoming empty and boring. The only thing man seems to be able to do all his life and remain sane and healthy is *work* (in the possibly idealized sense of sustained application of effort to purposive activity), even at the gently casual level on which we ordinarily operate.

But there are some energetic and irritating persons who are not satisfied with this easygoing arrangement. They not only drive themselves to ridiculous levels of activity, but they want to drive others too. They are the one-in-a-hundred or one-in-a-thousand who give more energy and time than anyone else is willing to give to keep the church going, or the lodge, or the union, or whatever cause or organization has won their loyalty. And by induction from their own devotion, they often stir the rest of us to a small additional percent of involvement.

These are the mobilizers, and it is their aim—as it is of some athletic coaches, some military commanders, some executives, some religious leaders—to try by every means they know to enlist from those around them the maximum exertion and commitment for the cause at hand. Once in a while, in the heat of combat or the crisis of a close game, they may succeed in rousing their fellows out of the sloth and self-indulgence into which they so readily sink (and which they enjoy so little), to a superhuman level of 75% or 80% exertion and involvement! And ever after, those so involved, despite their grumbling and groaning at the time, will proudly reminisce together over those intense and painful moments when they were really alive.

For that's what it means to *live:* to spend rather than to save ourselves, pouring out our vitality and vigor, our sweat and tears and blood, for what we believe: for meaning. That may be what was meant by the admonition, "he who saves his life will lose it"— since he who "saves" his life is already half-dead. The power generated by that intense commitment of human life in voluntary devotion to a cause is, in the long run, the *greatest power on earth.* And it is almost invariably harnessed, not by governments or industries, but by religious and quasi-religious movements.

No business can command the degree of devotion and involvement that religion (sometimes) can. No political party can either, except at campaign time, when it takes on a semireligious, almost evangelistic fervor. Television has seldom lifted the level of commitment of anyone, except possibly the performers, and that briefly. It can lower the level of commitment of spectators with the effectiveness of a shot of morphine. The mass media can shout and cajole and scold, but they really cannot do much to stir the basic shape of society beneath the surface sheen of shallow conformities.

The greatest mobilizers, who are usually religious leaders, like John Wesley, are persons who live near their maximum capacity not just for a few moments, but for years—not just for fame or wealth or sport, but for meaning. Is it any wonder that these dedicated, dynamic men and women, intensely and continuously so much more alive than anyone else, draw to themselves little groups of followers who want to share that abundant life?

These little bands of committed men and women have an impact on history out of all proportion to their numbers or apparent abilities. In the main, they are usually recruited from the least promising ranks of society: they are not noble or wealthy or well educated or particularly talented. All they have to offer is themselves, but that is more than others give to anything. For when a handful of wholly committed human beings give themselves fully to a great cause or faith, they are virtually irresistible. They cut through the partial and fleeting commitments of the rest of society like a buzz saw through peanut brittle.

They are able to do this for several reasons: (1) They are willing to put in more time and effort for their cause than most people do for even their fondest personal ambitions. (2) They have an assurance, a conviction of rightness, of being on the side of God, that most people in most human endeavors cannot match. (3) They are linked together in a band of mutually supportive, like-minded, equally devoted fellow believers, who reinforce one another in times of weakness, persecution, and doubt. (4) They are willing to subordinate their personal desires and ambitions to the shared goals of the group.

Meanings Are More than "Notions"

The way in which members of such committed groups are grasped by the meanings to which they are committed suggests that meanings are something more than mere ideas or concepts. Many philosophies offer neat, persuasive sets of ideas to explain the nature of reality and the duty and destiny of man, but it is a rare philosophy—if any—that will attract and hold a following of devoted, impassioned disciples who seek to pattern their own lives after it and to hand it on to their neighbors and their children. And if they do, it becomes more a religion than a philosophy, since this is the name we usually apply to an ideological group when it becomes a movement rather than a school. A German writer once observed: "Philosophy is the religion of the cultured: religion is the philosophy of the uncultured"—thereby neatly summing up the effective distinction between "meanings" and ideas. They appeal to different types of people as well as having very different effects.

The Quakers have a word for ideas that do not require anything of those who espouse them, but can be bandied back and forth like verbal playthings. They call them "notions." On the other hand, serious religious conversation about beliefs is expected to produce results: either a Yes or No from each participant. That is, meanings are addressed to persons and *demand* something from them: assent, commitment, adherence (or rejection). When used for detached, abstract speculation, they cease to be meanings and become mere notions: ideas that have lost the power to change lives, to recruit movements, to explain things convincingly. So we may hypothesize that: *meaning = concept + demand.*

In other words, there is a nonverbal element which accompanies the idea or concept to make it meaningful in the lives of perplexed persons. We want something more than a smooth, articulate verbal interpretation of what life is all about. Words are cheap; we want explanations that are validated by the commitment of other persons. "It's easy to *say* that, whatever happens, we should trust God, but how much do you trust God? What have you staked on it?" If the reply can be given, "I have staked my life on it," with convincing examples of what such trust has cost, then the explanation not only gains credibility but makes a corresponding demand upon the questioner: "What will *you* stake on it?"

There is as realistic an economy in the realm of meaning as in that of commodities, but the currency is different. In both cases, it obtains its value from the guarantees that undergird it: what has been invested in it, what backs it up. In the realm of meaning that backing, that guarantee or validation, is a personal and social earnestness shown in the investment by real people of time, money, effort, reputation, and self in the meaning and the movement that bears it. What costs nothing, accomplishes nothing. If it costs nothing to belong to such a community, it can't be worth much.

Meanings Are Borne by Movements

So the quality that enables religious meanings to take hold is not their rationality, their logic, their surface credibility, but rather the *demand* they make upon their adherents and the degree to which that demand is met by *commitment.* The most reasonable, most credible, most logical ideas in the world—without such demand and commitment—can never generate enough movement in human society to get one handcart over the hills to the Promised Land. But the Mormons did it—not one, but hundreds—with a commitment that transformed the lives of thousands, settled the wilderness of the Great Salt Lake, made the desert blossom like a rose, polygamously populated vast areas of the West, and persisted in polygamy for forty years despite decisions of the U.S. Supreme Court and expeditions of the U.S. Cavalry!

The concepts of the *Book of Mormon,* the *Doctrine and Covenants,* and the other sacred writings of the Church of Jesus Christ of Latter-day Saints are no more logical, reasonable, or credible than those of other religious movements—possibly less so. But these are evidently not the qualities that determine the effectiveness of religious meanings and the movements that bear them. The latter can apparently grow and flourish upon what would seem to many the most singular concepts. But more significant than the content of the faith for its success are the demands made upon would-be members and the commitment with which they respond.

For instance, not only do Mormons abstain from coffee, tea, and other stimulants, engage in extensive Temple-related rituals, and contribute substantially to the religious and welfare programs of the Church, but every young man who aspires to the upper priesthood (essentially a lay office, attained by a high proportion of Mormon men) must devote two years to full-time missionary activity at his own expense. This formidable requirement, far from discouraging new members, has not prevented the greatest rate of membership growth for any religious body of over a million members in this country: *5.6% per year* during the decade ending in 1968! Indeed, the point this chapter seeks to make is that the growth of membership of the Mormon Church occurs not *in spite of* its high demands upon its members but *because* of them. That is, no one would spend two years of his life propagating the meanings of Mormon religion if he did not consider them highly important. That is the real test of their depth and validity—not whether some gold plates were delivered to Joseph Smith by the Angel Moroni.

The gold plates of the Angel Moroni derive their convincingness from their place in a powerful stream of social experience in which thousands of individuals and families over more than a century have invested their time, money, effort, devotion, and their very lives. This stream of shared experience brings to members a system of explanations, a sacred cosmos (in Berger's terms) which makes life understandable to them, not by virtue of the system's inherent sense, but because it is validated by a tremendous and transforming movement which has lifted its followers out of their old homes and humdrum lives and told them who they are and what the world is all about and what they are to do about it. It is from mighty upheavals of the human spirit such as the Mormon migration rather than from books of philosophy that new resources of meaning are injected into tired societies, and perhaps only from such movements.

These upwellings of new meaning originate mainly among the lowliest ranks of society, not the loftiest. Inspired by a high demand that calls forth all they have, these sometimes unprepossessing little bands are lifted up in the scale of meaning until the whole society slopes down from them! That is, life has so much more significance to them than to even the wealthiest and most powerful that they, the humble believers, become in time the source, the touchstone, of understanding what it is all about.

This happened at the beginning of Christianity, when slaves and proletarians ("the filth and offscouring of the earth") were molded by their commitment to the meaning of their gospel into a force that outlived their well-born, all-powerful enemies, outlasted the Roman Empire, and shaped the outlook of half the world for more than a dozen centuries.

It happened in the Wesleyan revival, which made of former beggars and roustabouts such honest and self-respecting citizens that their neighbors took to entrusting to them the valuables they didn't trust themselves not to squander! Unfortunately, the virtues of Wesley's followers also helped them to prosper, and as they ascended in the esteem of their neighbors they tended to place their religious commitments in perspective with other concerns, which took on increasing importance. John Wesley, the founder of the movement, has summed up this process in what might be called Wesley's Law. *"Wherever riches have increased, the essence of religion has decreased in the same proportion.* Therefore, I do not see how it is possible, in the nature of things, for any revival of religion to continue long. For religion must necessarily produce both industry and frugality, and these cannot but produce riches. But as riches increase, so will pride, anger, and love of the world in all its branches. . . . *Is there no way to prevent this—this continual decay of pure religion?"*[2]

This well describes the mechanism by which the level of demand is lowered, the inner conviction of religious meaning ebbs away, and its institutions decline. The question this study asks is Wesley's question: Is there no way to prevent this decay of pure religion?

To understand the process of decay as it affects the institutions of religion, let us consider the *ideal type* of a religious group that is vigorously and effectively making sense of life for its members. If we could combine the outstanding characteristics of the most energetic and dynamic religious groups into a composite systematic description, what would we see?

2. Quoted in Weber, *op. cit.*, p. 175 (emphasis added).

Chapter V

Traits of a "Strong" Religion

Those who are accustomed to the placid and circumspect ways of the mainline Protestant denominations in America today may not think of religion as a strenuous and fateful adventure, catching up men's lives in a surge of significance and purpose, changing the very definition of what it is to be a man worthy of respect, and thus shifting upward a whole society's expectations of human behavior. But religion has often been this kind of movement in the past and will be in the future.

Therefore we should not be content with an idea of it that accepts as its norm the dilute residue of former vitality which is all that remains of religion in many people's lives. Instead, we should take as a standard what religion can be in its purest, most intense and concentrated form, just as a chemist seeks to isolate the purest form of an element he is trying to study and understand. In order to know what to look for, however, and what methods of purification to use, he must form some idea of what the element is, and his advance hypothesis is then sustained, rejected, or modified by what he finds.

In a similar approach, let us try to imagine an ideal type of what religion might be in its most concentrated form, a model of a religious group that would have maximum cohesion, vitality, and functional effectiveness. Then we can see if there are historical specimens which substantiate this hypothesis or whether it must be modified or rejected. In constructing such a model, let us hang it on three dimensions which would be useful and applicable in describing any organization. We may label them "goals," "controls," and "communication," referring respectively to three sets of questions about any organization.[1]

1. *Goals*
   a. What are the organization's aims, purposes, objectives, central convictions, creed, ideology, "explanation" of life (these are meant to be similar and overlapping features)?
   b. How are these goals determined?
   c. What place do they hold in the lives of members? That is, what demand do they make upon members? And what commitment is given in response?
2. *Controls*
   a. How are the organization's requirements, standards, or rules enforced?
   b. What sanctions are available? How strictly are they applied?
   c. What is the incidence and frequency of deviance? How is it handled?
   d. What discipline will members accept without leaving the group?
3. *Communication*
   a. How does the group communicate its beliefs, its standards, to members (internal) and to others (external)?
   b. How does it deal with messages (from outside) that differ from its own?

In our model religious group, we could expect such firm adherence of members to the group's beliefs that they would be willing to suffer persecution, to sacrifice status, possessions, safety, and life itself for the organization, its convictions, its goals. We would see wholehearted *commitment* on the part of members, each individual's goals being highly or wholly identified with—or derived from—those of the group, so that a shoulder-to-shoulder solidarity

1. These dimensions have been chosen rather arbitrarily and are not the only ones that could be used to describe organizations. Nevertheless, they are not without rationale or precedent in the literature.

would enable it to withstand all onslaughts from without and avoid betrayal from within.

Moreover, members would willingly and fully submit themselves to the *discipline* of the group, obeying the decisions of the leadership without cavil and accepting punishment for infractions without resentment, considering any sanction preferable to being expelled.

Lastly, the model religious organization would be marked by an irrepressible *missionary zeal,* an eagerness to tell the Good News to others, with warmth and confidence and winsomeness in the telling, refusing to be silenced even by repression or persecution. A virtual flood of outgoing communications would be matched by a high degree of reverberance within. That is, members would be continually giving and receiving messages among themselves about the group's goals, its daily life, the progress of other members, and so on; new members and the young would be constantly bathed in a nurturing stream of such communications, often in a kind of in-group code, a special terminology peculiar to the group and less intelligible to outsiders.

CHART A: EVIDENCES OF SOCIAL STRENGTH

GOALS	CONTROLS	COMMUNICATION
1. *Commitment* —willingness to sacrifice status, possessions, safety, life itself, for the cause or the company of the faithful —a total response to a total demand —group solidarity —total identification of individual's goals with group's	2. *Discipline* —willingness to obey the commands of (charismatic) leadership without question —willingness to suffer sanctions for infraction rather than leave the group	3. *Missionary Zeal* —eagerness to tell the "good news" of one's experience of salvation to others —refusal to be silenced (Acts 5:26) —internal communications stylized and highly symbolic: a cryptic language —winsomeness

These traits have been listed in the accompanying chart, with subdivisions under each of the three social dimensions, respectively labeled: (1) "Commitment," (2) "Discipline," and (3) "Missionary Zeal." There are probably other evidences that could be listed, but these should suffice to lead us into a general recognition of what the syndrome of social strength would be. There are also many other admirable virtues in human life which do not necessarily conduce so directly to social strength.

This model of a religious organization of maximum social strength is not difficult to match with empirical examples. There have been many such groups in history, as the reader is doubtless aware. Several will be briefly described to give texture and verisimilitude to the model. They are: (a) the Anabaptist movement, (b) the Wesleyan revival, (c) the Mormon migration, and (d) Jehovah's Witnesses. Many others might have been chosen, including some non-Western, non-Christian examples. But these are selected because American readers are likely to be more familiar with them from their own experience.

The Anabaptist Movement

The Anabaptists were little bands of believing brethren who sprang up on the left wing of the Protestant Reformation in the sixteenth century. The name means "rebaptizers" and was applied to them by their enemies because rebaptizing was an offense punishable by death.[2] The guiding principle among them was to restore the original Christian Church of the New Testament (as they understood it from their study of the Scriptures). They rejected many of the features of both Rome and the Protestant churches (Lutheran and Calvinist) as perversions of the Gospel and banded together in little conventicles to recreate the True Church.

Their only authority was the Gospel as understood by the congregation of believers, made up entirely and exclusively of those who wholly subscribed to it, not just in theory but in practice. They

2. See especially Franklin H. Littell, *The Origins of Sectarian Protestantism* (New York: Macmillan Co., 1964), whose definition of authentic Anabaptism is accepted here. The name was applied to a wide range of radical religious groups in Europe, including violent revolutionaries (as in Münster) and antinomian individualistic "spiritualizers" like Franck and Schwenkfeld. Littell limits the term to the disciplined elements between these extremes, viz.: Swiss Brethern, Hutterites, South German Brethren, and Dutch Mennonites (p. 45).

rejected the validity of force as a determinant in religion and insisted that the magistrate (the state) has no authority in matters of faith—a truly revolutionary teaching for that time, or even for today, which resulted in persecution, exile, and death for those who taught and lived such defiance of the powers that be.

Though obedient to the magistrate with respect to matters not connected with faith, the Anabaptists made religion such a pervasive part of their lives—as did the magistrate, at least in a cultural and legal sense—that there was no lack of occasion for conflict. Because this official had the duty of exercising compulsion in matters religious, Anabaptists could not be magistrates or the servants of magistrates (soldiers), nor would they take the oath required of vassals. Theirs was a stance, not so much of pacifism as of nonresistance, both to lawless evil and to the lawful yet coercive power of the magistrate. They opposed violent revolution as they did violent persecution, offering only martyrdom as their final answer to either. And martyrdom they had abundant opportunity to endure.

They rejected completely the marriage between church and state that had taken place under Constantine, believing that it had seduced the church into reliance on power, wealth, and prestige. They rejected all pomp, ostentation, formalism, and hierarchical officialdom in the church. Instead, they followed a humble and unpretentious style of life, sharing whatever they had with each other, even to the "common-ism" of Hutterite communities.

They rejected infant baptism because it was the device by which myriads were brought into the church who had not knowingly and willingly taken upon themselves the discipleship commanded by the Gospel. Thus the church was filled with pagans whose baptism was spurious, and it was therefore no church in the New Testament sense. The only true church, they held, is one in which believers' baptism is the only entrance, the mutual admonition of the brethren the only wall, and the ban the only rod.

The ban (*Meidung*) is the "spiritual government" of the Anabaptist movement. A member who violates the rules of the church is cut off from all personal contact with his fellow church members, including his family and friends. He is shunned; no one speaks to him or recognizes his presence. Though given food, clothing, and shelter (as even a non-Christian in need would be), he is denied participation as a member in the group whose esteem means most to him. Only by contrite submission can he obtain forgiveness and restoration to full membership again.

This sanction sounds austere indeed, and can be devastating in its full impact, but without it there is no way to maintain the discipline of the True Church. At its best it is not an arbitrary or authoritarian penalty. To begin with, the standards of the church are known to the member when he accepts baptism, as a willing adult, after extensive preparation. New standards, or modifications of the old, are arrived at by the whole congregation, in which every member has an equal voice and none but members any voice at all—a form of truly participatory democracy bodied forth in Anabaptism at a time when no democracy whatever existed in state or church. In relative reasonableness, the members through discussion search the Word of God for guidance. Only when a consensus is reached—not just a majority vote but general agreement—is the Holy Spirit felt to have communicated to the congregation the way it ought to go.

After the consensus is reached, however, no one departs from it without risking the ban, unless the congregation reaches a new consensus. This sanction is undertaken by the congregation in love and sorrow rather than anger or vengefulness. It is not so much a withdrawal of the group from the offending member as a recognition that *he* has withdrawn himself from them by his offense, and until he has returned they cannot pretend he is still among them. A person either belongs or he doesn't. If he does belong, he must meet the standards. If he doesn't meet them, he no longer belongs.

The Anabaptists also believed that the members in good standing were *accountable for one another.* That is, if they saw a member beginning to go astray, it was their duty to remonstrate with him and encourage him in righteousness. If he was ill or in need, it was their duty to care for him and supply his needs as best they could. To this day among the Amish—a strict and primitivist form of Anabaptism—there are no Amishmen on welfare, imprisoned for felonies, or hospitalized for mental illness; they look after their own.

Furthermore, since all members of the congregation participate in reaching the consensus, all must be able to understand the Word of God on which the congregation's life is based. Thus every member was taught to read the Bible for himself—the beginning of universal common education centuries before public schools were invented. Every member was also expected to contribute his full share to the welfare of the congregation, though only the Hutterites held all goods in common, and still do. If any would not share, the Lord's Supper would not be shared with him.

Anabaptists were very serious about the Lord's Supper. They felt that harm might come to anyone who took the Supper while unworthy: not only might he be punished, but the whole congregation might suffer. For that reason (among others) they refused to participate in the Mass of the established churches, where unbelievers partook as well as believers, where the good and the evil were not separated, where no "spiritual government" was in effect and yet all went to Mass alike. So far as possible, they tried to avoid close relationships with unbelievers (non-Anabaptists.) They would do business with them and tried to be good neighbors, but did not enter into friendship, partnership, or marriage.

Unlike the territorial churches of their time—Catholic, Lutheran, or Reformed—into which every resident was received by baptism as soon as possible after birth, the Anabaptists were indefatigable missionaries. While the Reformers were insisting (as a condition of mutual nonaggression) that only the Apostles had been told to go forth into the whole world and preach the Gospel to every creature, the Anabaptists "were among the first to make the Commission binding upon *all church members*" (Littell, p. 112). As though life were not hazardous enough for them, even if they lay low at home where they had friends and knew the terrain, they insisted on going out into new territory to spread the Word, sticking their necks out wherever they went to tell the Good News. They did so fully expecting to suffer for their faith, and they were seldom disappointed.

In several Swiss cantons their property was confiscated; hundreds of special police were appointed to track them down or hound them out of the territory. For the crime of rebaptizing many were executed by drowning without trial or hearing. Others were thrown into prison, burned, or hanged. Whoever accepted leadership often also accepted an early and violent death.

Although persecuted everywhere it went in Europe and almost stamped out in South Germany, the movement continued to grow and spread. Borne by exiles, journeymen, missionaries, it seeped under the most rigid barriers, defied the most vehement threats, and survived the most virulent persecutions that the combined powers of church and state could bring against it.

Not only does Anabaptism still continue in varying degrees of fidelity among many descendants (Amish, Mennonites, Hutterites, and various companies of Brethren), but to it we owe new understandings of what Christianity can be. Many important elements now widely accepted in Western civilization are attributable to them: no civil coercion in religious matters, separation of church and state, common universal education, and self-government within a community of equals. Others we have not yet accepted but may succeed in doing so some day: nonviolence, unostentation, mutual help, "living loose from the world."

The Wesleyan Revival

In the eighteenth century England was suffering from moral anemia. Poverty, vice, drunkenness, injustice, and corruption were everywhere. The churches were empty and the jails full. In 1750 over eleven billion gallons of gin were consumed in England, much of it in circumstances similar to those portrayed by William Hogarth in "Gin Lane" and other paintings. The Church of England had over eleven thousand livings in the kingdom—positions for clergymen paid from state revenues—of which six thousand were occupied by men who did not deign to go near the parishes they were paid to serve, but farmed them out to poorly paid curates and themselves went to live luxuriously in London or on the Continent.

Crime flourished despite inhumanly savage penalties, such as hanging for stealing a loaf of bread, or cutting off the hand of a pickpocket. Orphans, foundlings, and paupers were the responsibility of the churchwardens, whose Christian solicitude for their charges was such that, according to the parish registry of Greater London for 1750–55, in many of the "workhouses" all the children died within a year of admission.

In this rather dismal setting, John and Charles Wesley began their ministry to the unchurched. Though they were priests of the Church of England, the doors of most churches were barred to them because of their "emotional" and "enthusiastic" preaching. So they preached to the poor on streetcorners, in open fields, in prisons (the poor were not in the churches anyway). Their gatherings in the open were often broken up by rowdies who threw stones at the speakers and drove cattle through the throngs. The lives of the brothers were often imperiled by mobs, sometimes stirred up by angry clergy of the established church who resented being shown up in their own parishes. The Wesleys were denounced by the press of the period, ridiculed in cartoons, and discredited by other clergymen, but the poor flocked to hear them and became members of the Methodist societies they founded.

John Wesley, a man of slight stature and frail health, frequently preached to thousands of miners as they emerged from the collieries. Although exhausted after twelve or more hours of work in the mines, they would crowd around to hear him tell them that God cared about *them* even if they didn't go to church, that Christ had died for *them,* that they could be saved from sin by the love of God—until the tears ran rivulets in the coal dust on their cheeks.

Rejected by the established church, though not seeking to depart from it, the Methodists (as they were called in contempt) met in private homes for weekly "class meetings," at which—poor and unlettered though most of them were—they sang and prayed together, confessed their sins, and encouraged one another in righteousness. One of the members was designated class leader, and it was his duty to look after the moral progress of the others and admonish and caution each one personally every week. By such means, men and women who had been living in hopeless desperation found themselves bound together in an earnest and meaningful organization which cared what they did with their lives and shepherded them in times of temptation or distress.

John Wesley could not be everywhere to look after his followers throughout the land—though he tried, traveling incessantly from dawn till dark, preaching several times a day, writing or reading on horseback or in coach, checking over the class leaders' records on the condition of their charges' souls. To help him nourish the spiritual needs of his thousands upon thousands of followers, Wesley put lay preachers at the head of clusters of classes. Though at first they were little better than those they were sent to lead, in time they became true moral and spiritual guides for some of the neediest people in the land, thanks in large part to the close supervision of Wesley and the books of instruction on all subjects (including medical advice) which he wrote for them while jogging across England and then had printed on a press set up in an old foundry.

Under this diligent tutelage, the followers of the Wesleys became noted for their honesty, thrift, industry, and zeal. Many who had been drunkards and petty thieves became sober and hardworking pillars of their classmeetings. As we have noted already, their unregenerate neighbors would often confide their savings to them for safekeeping, trusting the Methodists more than they trusted themselves. In time they became self-respecting and respected, as the pressures of despair drained away and they found new meaning and purpose for their lives.[3]

The Mormon Migration[4]

It was in 1830 in western New York State (often called the "burned-over district" for its succession of religious revivals) that

3. See J. W. Bready, *England Before and After Wesley* (New York: Harper & Brothers, n.d.).

4. Much of this historical material is derived from an excellent sociological study by Thomas F. O'Dea, *The Mormons* (Chicago: University of Chicago Press, 1957).

Joseph Smith, then twenty-six, published *The Book of Mormon,* claiming to have translated it from plates of gold supplied by a spirit named Moroni, son of the original compiler, Mormon.

Around this document Smith gathered a small group of followers, which soon grew large enough to send missionaries to neighboring states. By 1833, twelve hundred of the "Saints" were living in Missouri, where they began to incur the hostility of the "gentiles" because of their assertion of a divine mandate to occupy the land, their friendly attitude toward the Indians, their suspected abolitionism, and their solidarity and industriousness, which enabled them to prosper and buy more land.

Before long violence broke out, the Mormon printing plant was destroyed, the leaders tarred and feathered. The Saints appealed to the courts and the governor for protection, but this did not prevent their being driven out of Independence by a mob in a November storm. Losing most of their property there, they moved north to Clay County, Missouri to make a new start. Welcomed at first by the residents, they prospered for three years, but then their new neighbors also turned against them, envious of their success and resentful of their solidarity and claims of divine endorsement. So again they moved, this time to Ray County, Missouri, which was virtually unsettled. Here they bought a large tract of land, and the legislature granted them permission to form a new county, whose seat, Far West, was laid out on a plan drawn by Smith.

Here once more they prospered. Six hundred Saints from the East joined them. Converts began to arrive from England and later from Scandinavia and other countries. Mormon settlements spread into three adjoining counties, again rousing gentile fears. But this time the Mormons were not inclined to turn the other cheek. By June 1838 a secret corps of militant men was organized, called the Sons of Dan, Destroying Angels, or "Danite" bands, both to defend the Saints against outside aggression and to keep a rein on internal dissension, which was a continuous though never quite fatal problem. A steady stream of apostates abandoned the faith over the years, including several from the highest ranks. Around the nucleus of the Danite bands a militia was organized, called the Host of Israel. Preparing for trouble, they were soon obliged by the gentiles.

In August, Mormons were prevented from voting at Gallatin in Davies County, resulting in a riot in which the Saints got the upper hand. On October 29, seventeen Mormons were killed and fifteen wounded at Haun's Mill, whereupon the state militia marched on Far West with orders from the governor to drive the Mormons out or exterminate them. Outnumbered, the Saints capitulated. Smith and other leaders went to jail for a brief time, and some eight thousand Mormons, salvaging what little they could, moved across the Mississippi eastward into Illinois.

That state welcomed them and in 1840 granted them a special charter for a new city, Nauvoo, which they began to build again from Smith's plan for the City of Zion, on land purchased at a bend in the Mississippi. The Nauvoo Charter made it almost an independent kingdom, with its own courts, university, militia, and artillery. Joseph Smith was commissioned Lieutenant General of a body of more than one thousand men.

Here several new revelations were announced by Smith, the president, "prophet, seer, and revelator" of the Church. Here he first revealed to some of the inner circle of leaders the new doctrine of plural marriage, which they began to practice in secret while denying vehemently that any such thing existed. This innovation was a main cause of the defection of two Mormon leaders, William Law and Robert Foster, who charged Smith publicly with being a false prophet. He in turn excommunicated them and had the rebels' printing press destroyed by the Nauvoo Legion. Law and Foster fled to Carthage, Illinois, where they filed suit against Smith and his followers.

Around this conflict all the accumulated hostilities on both sides coalesced. The Mormons, having been hounded out of Missouri, had at last found their Zion of virtual independence and did not propose to be driven out again. Their experiences had strengthened their solidarity as a group and increased their separateness from non-Mormons, who resented their "arrogance," "pretensions," and growing truculence. Both sides began to mobilize for war. Demands were made upon the governor to call out the militia; he hurried to Carthage and found it already assembled, summoned by local authorities. Trying to avoid open warfare, he notified Smith that if he would surrender himself for trial in Carthage, he (the governor) would guarantee his safety.

Smith thought of escaping to the west and even set out across the river from Nauvoo, but changed his mind and came back to surrender. He had the Nauvoo Legion give up the weapons that belonged to the state, but they kept those paid for by Mormons. The prophet and three other leaders were then jailed in Carthage to await trial. Governor Ford disbanded the militia and went to Nauvoo to reassure the Mormons. While he was away, on June 27, 1844, 150 members of the supposedly disbanded militia broke into the jail and slaughtered Joseph Smith and his brother Hyrum. The surrounding countryside girded for defense against avenging Mormons, but the Saints were too shaken and sorrowful to seek vengeance. After burying their dead, they voted unanimously to leave punishment to the courts.

After a lull, the friction between the Mormons and their neighbors resumed. In 1845 the legislature repealed the Nauvoo Charter, and bands of gentiles burned Mormon houses, barns, and grain throughout the country. This led to retaliatory raids, and it was soon open warfare again, with artillery used on both sides. But the Mormons realized they could not fight the whole state of Illinois and agreed to leave Nauvoo and the new temple they had just completed. They asked for sufficient time to dispose of their property and find a new location to the west, but their exodus seemed too slow to their adversaries and the city was besieged by an armed mob. As the last Mormons crossed the river, looking back they could see their new temple and parts of their former city in flames. Once again the Chosen People were on the move.

Joseph Smith's successor was Brigham Young, who organized the westward trek that began when two thousand Mormons left Nauvoo on February 4, 1846 in twenty-below-zero weather. After four and a half months of muddy struggle across Iowa they reached Council Bluffs on the Missouri River, where they started a temporary settlement, calling it Winter Quarters (now Omaha, Nebraska). On the way they built bridges and planted crops for those who were to follow. By the end of summer, between 10,000 and 15,000 Mormons had crossed Iowa and were gathered at Winter Quarters. In April, 1847 Brigham Young set out for the Great Salt Lake with the first party of 148 persons.

On July 7, when they reached Fort Bridger, Young fell ill with mountain fever and had to travel the rest of the way in a wagon, while an advance party under Orson Pratt hunted out the best way down into the Great Salt Lake valley. On July 24, 1847 Young reached a point where he could see the valley. Recognizing it from an earlier vision, he announced, "This is the right place." A city was laid out, following Joseph Smith's plan for the City of Zion, which is now Salt Lake City.

It was relatively barren and uninviting territory, with very low rainfall, which was why Young chose it in preference to California or Oregon: he wanted a haven for the Mormons that no one else wanted, and Utah was it. Realizing that nothing would grow without irrigation, the Mormon leaders had given thought to the problem before they reached Salt Lake. Within a few hours of their arrival, Young had announced that there would be no private ownership of streams of water, a potato crop was planted, and work was begun on a community ditch to provide water for all in the city.

In the next ten years, 95 Mormon communities were scattered through the valley, most of them settled by families sent out by the Church leadership to develop irrigable valleys, which soon began to carpet the arid territory with green. In the second decade another 135 settlements were added, with some 20,000 European converts arriving to occupy them. By the time Brigham Young died in 1877, there were about 140,000 Mormons in the Territory of Utah, many of whom had travelled from Europe in expeditions organized by Mormon agents, financed by the Church's Perpetual Emigrating Fund. In 1856, when crop failure cut short its financial resources, Young designed a handcart that immigrants could pull across the plains to transport their belongings. This plan worked well for three groups that year, but two later companies were overtaken by winter, the breakdown of carts made of inferior wood, and illness; 75 out of 400 died in one group, 150 out of 576 in the other.

The great migration, which continued for years, was managed with efficiency and discipline. Both leaders and followers in the Church cooperated vigorously to sustain the pilgrims when they reached the Promised Land. But their final test was still to come. After having conquered the environment over a decade of struggle, they were once again faced with their old problem of outsiders.

Beginning with the California Gold Rush in 1849, which drew a flood of prospectors across Utah, and increasing with the completion of the railroad in 1869, a stream of gentiles settled among the Saints. Though a small minority, and still a minority in Utah today, they were vocal in their complaints against Mormon dominance and cohesiveness. In 1850, Congress created the Territory of Utah with Brigham Young as its first governor, but about half of the territorial officers were non-Mormons who were not sympathetic to the cause of Zion.

There was an effort to bind the Saints more tightly together during the famine of 1854–55, when missionaries from the central leadership went to every settlement and interviewed each member individually about his sins and his loyalty to the Church. The result was heightened emotion and enthusiasm among the Saints, increased tension with the gentiles. "Brigham's Avenging Angels," Bill Hickman and Orin Porter Rockwell, are said to have terrorized apostates and gentile troublemakers.

At this juncture, President Buchanan decided to replace Young as governor with a gentile, and sent 2,500 troops to Utah to keep order. The result was Utah's "Mormon War." The Mormons followed a scorched-earth policy of withdrawal as the federal troops advanced. At great sacrifice, border settlements were evacuated on Brigham's orders, their buildings and crops burned to deny them to the "enemy." Perhaps 30,000 Mormons packed their belongings and set out for southern Utah. In that part of the state the culminating event took place: an emigrant party of outspokenly anti-Mormon gentiles was attacked by Mormons and their Indian allies, who killed 120 men and women, sparing only 17 small children.

The "Mountain Meadows Massacre" horrified both Mormons and gentiles and led to the end of the Mormon War. Brigham Young met with a peace commission from the President and received a pardon for his "rebellion." A new governor was appointed and a legislature elected, but the members of the legislature continued to meet with Brigham Young and to follow his advice rather than that of the official territorial governor. A boycott against gentile and apostate merchants was proclaimed by the Church in the mid-sixties but was not effective, since the Church could no longer enforce among its members the necessary discipline.

The main bone of contention between Mormons and gentiles, however, was polygamy. It did not reach its climax until after Brigham Young's death. He had announced the new doctrine to the general membership of the Church in 1852, when it caused some distress but no disruption. Gradually it became a central doctrine of the Church and was practiced by many of the leading Mormons (at least by those who could afford it).

The rest of the nation became increasingly scandalized by this teaching and practice, and in 1862 Congress passed a law against it, which however was not effective in Utah as no grand jury there would indict. When a conviction was at last obtained in 1875, the territorial court voided it. When the case was appealed to the U.S. Supreme Court, it held, in a famous decision in *U.S.* v. *Reynolds,* that Congress could outlaw polygamy and that the plea of religious freedom was not sufficient to excuse violation of that law.

As the 1880's began, President Hayes and then President Arthur announced that they would make every effort to end polygamy. Federal officers attempted to detect and apprehend the leading practitioners of plural marriage, but their efforts were hindered by the Mormon underground—a concerted conspiracy by Church members to conceal suspects and assist them to escape to remote areas of Utah or to Mexico or Canada. The Church leaders headed this resistance, with Mormon president John Taylor going into hiding, where he died in 1887, adamant to the end.

Despite this resistance, 573 men were convicted of plural marriage. Congress in 1887 disincorporated the Church of Jesus Christ of Latter-day Saints, and over $1,000,000 in property (including $400,000 in cash) was taken from the Church in fines and penalties. The Mormons had petitioned Congress for statehood since 1850, but it became clear that Utah would never be admitted to the Union as long as polygamy continued. So in 1890 Taylor's successor as president of the Church, Wilford Woodruff, issued an official declaration urging Mormons to submit to the federal laws against polygamy and to end the practice.

Since 1890, the Church has officially opposed polygamy as a practice, though it remains a theological teaching. It has even excommunicated Mormon fundamentalists who clung to the old tradition of plural marriage and continued to practice it. But there survives to this day a clandestine and recusant remnant of several thousand polygamists hidden in the backwaters of Mormon society. Members of such a community in Short Creek, Arizona, were recently prosecuted for polygamy.

Thus, after some forty or fifty years of unswerving persistence in its "peculiarity," the Mormon Church at last acceded to the pressures of the surrounding society. Since 1890 it has ceased to be a movement, a nation-within-the-nation, and has become another church among many. Yet the momentum from the heroic period persists: the exclusiveness with respect to other religious groups, the missionary emphasis, the tithing, the abstinence from stimulants, the membership growth, all bespeak a rich deposit of meaning that still actuates a vigorous organization today.

Jehovah's Witnesses[5]

The organization known since 1931 as Jehovah's Witnesses began obscurely—as most religious movements do—in 1872, when Charles Taze Russell, then twenty, gathered together "a few Chris-

5. Much of this material is derived from Herbert H. Stroup's study *The Jehovah's Witnesses* (New York: Columbia University Press, 1945).

tian persons in a little house in Pennsylvania to consider the Scriptures relative to the coming of Christ and His Kingdom." By 1884 he had sufficient followers to organize Zion's Watch Tower Society, which in 1909 moved its headquarters to Brooklyn, where it is now known as the Watch Tower Bible and Tract Society.

Under Russell's leadership, the movement grew and spread abroad to England and other countries. The entire early literature of the movement originated with him, and he was in great demand as a speaker until his death in 1916. His place was taken shortly thereafter by Joseph F. Rutherford, chief legal counsel for the society, who in turn became the unquestioned leader, spokesman, and sole author for the movement until his death in 1942. His successor is Nathan H. Knorr, former vice-president, who directs the worldwide activities of the Witnesses today from their Brooklyn headquarters.

Those activities consist primarily of door-to-door distribution of literature and playing of phonograph recordings of "Judge" Rutherford's works produced at the Brooklyn printing plant. (Russell's writings seem to have disappeared from the canon of Watch Tower holy writ.) Selling Bible-study materials from door-to-door and on street-corners may seem a prosaic and pedestrian mode of religious behavior, yet around it has grown a movement of surprising vigor and intensity. Or perhaps it would be more accurate to say that colporteuring is the visible objective of an active and meaningful social experience.

Hundreds of thousands of Jehovah's Witnesses spend every hour they can spare outside their regular jobs as part-time colporteurs (these are called Publishers). Thousands spend full time organizing, teaching, and leading them (these are called Pioneers). Meticulous records are kept of books and pamphlets distributed, call-backs to be made on interested prospects, Bible-study sessions scheduled, Watch-Tower subscriptions sold, and so forth. The high points of the movement are its annual conventions, attended by hundreds of thousands of Witnesses from all over the world. Yankee Stadium in New York has been the scene of several such huge events, when the grounds are even more crowded than for the World Series, but left immaculate by the impressively disciplined throngs.

Among many other remarkable things, Witnesses believe that Christ is coming again soon to destroy Satan's organization, which now dominates the earth. All earthly corporate bodies, including churches and governments, are part of that demonic structure; therefore Witnesses owe them no allegiance and should have no part of them. For this reason, they refuse to salute the flag or to serve in the armies of nations. Their only duty on earth is to *witness* to the coming of God's Judgment: both to *watch*—in the sense that no human effort can hasten or delay it; and to *testify* to its coming, so that men may be aware of what is happening—not that they can save themselves thereby, since no one knows who will be saved. Consequently, the Witnesses have and need no elaborate rituals or sacred days, deeming these the trappings of religion, which is part of Satan's organization. They also refuse blood transfusions, since the Bible prohibits the "eating of blood," and to their way of thinking a transfusion is essentially an ingestion. Witnesses also reject the Trinity, hell, and several other traditional Christian beliefs.

In fidelity to these few simple and eminently reasonable convictions the Jehovah's Witnesses have fallen afoul of governments and churches in many lands. Imprisoned and sometimes executed by states as diverse as Spain, South Africa, Greece, Sudan, and the Soviet Union, they can count their martyrs in the hundreds, perhaps thousands. In the United States, efforts to ban their canvassing, silence their phonographs, and make them salute the flag, accept blood transfusions, or serve in the armed forces have generated a succession of court cases that have done much to shape the jurisprudence spelling out and safeguarding the free exercise of religion—no small achievement for a movement which claims not to be one!

Members of the group meet weekly in simple, bare buildings called Kingdom Halls to report on their week's work, encourage one another to greater efforts, and get their supplies and quota for the next week from the service director (a full-time lay officer who in another organization might be called a clergyman[6]). According to Stroup and others, they are avid in their thirst for every new impartation of doctrine from headquarters, every new shred of biblical interpretation that will help them in their efforts to persuade others to the faith.

Leaders of the organization are assigned from headquarters, paid a subsistence wage, and expected to put in every waking hour in the cause—and they generally do. No criticism of the leadership is permitted; dissidents are immediately dropped from the movement. Unlike the Mormons, the Witnesses seem to show little interest in divergent views and little disposition to find fault with leaders. (In fact, the leaders are little more than names—if that—to the rank and file.) Rather, Witnesses seem not only obedient but unquestioningly grateful for the opportunity to obey.

Stroup paraphrases an attorney of the American Civil Liberties Union who had handled many Witnesses' court cases, and warned him what to expect. "Probably you have never seen anyone who is willing actually to die for his religious convictions. With our sophisticated ways of doing things, and with our mentalities which never seem to deal with absolute certainties, we moderns think that there is nothing for which a man should give his life. But when you meet the Witnesses, you will be meeting, probably for the first time, people who are willing to be persecuted, even slain, for the sake of their religious faith." Stroup adds, "At that time I was not entirely convinced. Now I am. I am confident that the Witnesses demonstrate one of the most sacrificial ways of living which has been seen in many decades" (p. 63).

An attractive, sweet, intelligent, vivacious high school girl was won away from the (Methodist) church of which I was pastor by a group of Jehovah's Witnesses who came to her home for Bible study one or two evenings a week *for months* until she joined them. Her parting words about the church she was leaving were:

6. Stroup says, however, that there are no "members" properly speaking; they are all (equally) Jehovah's Witnesses. That is, they believe, and have insisted in court, that they are all equivalent to ministers as defined by Selective Service laws.

"I wish *your* church was one-tenth as serious about *its* message as *they* are about theirs!"

Dr. Stroup mentions several other characteristics of the group. One is their unique vocabulary. "Following his conversion, the believer enters upon a discipline designed to form him according to the image of the ideal Witness. He receives a new vocabulary, with new meanings, which in the course of time become habitual, and are the same for all. Witnesses do not try to express their ideas in ways of their own, but employ fixed word patterns constituting the official parlance of the movement. Should anyone not follow these patterns, his orthodoxy is quickly and seriously questioned" (p. 101).

Another trait is their relationship to other groups. "[The Witness] must also 'sever all relations with the world' . . . . Opposition to other churches is a condition of witnessing: all 'true' Witnesses are expected soon after conversion to cancel their church membership, if they hold any. . ." (pp. 102–3). Even family relationships are subsidiary to the faith. If the spouse is not receptive to conversion, the Witness is often encouraged to separation, though not to divorce, which is frowned upon. Even if the spouse is receptive, this does not insure companionship in service, as the two may be sent on separate missions, or one may be active while the other must stay home to look after the children (pp. 116 ff.).

The believer who is troubled by debts or other obligations incurred before conversion is advised that such ties no longer bind, since he has died to the old self which made those commitments (p. 112). Many part-time Witnesses are unhappy in the secular occupations that provide their livelihood and long to spend all their time witnessing. Just as the movement seeks to encompass all of the believer's life, so does its ideology purport to encompass all questions.

[It] does not attempt to make a partial inquiry into the nature of reality, but claims to have succeeded already in obtaining the final answer to all important religious problems. One of the delights of Witnesses is to state proudly that there is no question which they cannot answer successfully. . . . [P. 124]

The acceptance of the theology of the movement is a matter of "all or none". . . . He cannot choose part of the Lutheran creed and part of the

Witness belief. . . . Immediately upon conversion, the neophyte declares himself in harmony with all the beliefs of the organization whether he understands them or not—and often he has not even heard of some of them. . . . [P. 125]

The will to believe is so great among Witnesses that the content of belief becomes incidental. . . . [P. 127]

One gets the impression . . . that they could just as well manage all that they are doing for and receiving from the movement if some other absolutist theology were to be substituted. [P. 138][7]

Many other religious movements might be described. There is much more that could be said about these four, and numerous other sources could be cited for each. However, what is needed here is not a comprehensive historical treatment so much as a quick sketch of four strong religious movements to compare with the model suggested earlier.

7. Cf. Eric Hoffer, *The True Believer* (New York: Harper & Row, 1951), who holds that all mass movements draw from the same reservoir of susceptible followers and are therefore readily interchangeable (pp. 14 ff.).

Chapter VI

Why Not a Strong Ecumenical Religion?

If the exposition in the preceding chapter has been successful, it will have left at least two impressions. The religious movements described have often seemed almost superhuman in their dynamism, their expansiveness, their endurance, their impact on individuals and on history. And living in close proximity to such movements, trying to get along with their members, can be strenuous, if not intensely irritating. Such has indeed been the experience of "gentiles" in Salt Lake City, the Anglican squires of Wesleyan England, and anyone who has been visited by uninvited but determined Jehovah's Witnesses in the middle of Christmas morning!

Traits of Strictness

We cannot avoid noticing that in addition to the evidences of social strength which I have listed in Row A of our model, there seem to be in our specimens certain corresponding traits of what could be called strictness (Chart B).

4. *Absolutism.* If the members of a religious group show high commitment to its goals or beliefs, and willingness to suffer and sacrifice for them, etc., they also tend to show a kind of absolutism about those aims, beliefs, explanations of life. One would think that knowledge began with them, that all other attempts to explain

CHART B: TRAITS OF STRICTNESS

GOALS	CONTROLS	COMMUNICATION	
4. *Absolutism* —belief that "we have the Truth and all others are in error" —closed system of meaning and value which explains everything —uncritical and unreflective attachment to a single set of values	5. *Conformity* —intolerance of deviance or dissent —"shunning" of outcasts (*Meidung*) —shared stigmata of belonging (Quaker garb and plain talk) —group confessions or criticism (Oneida) —separatism	6. *Fanaticism* (outflow > inflow)	
		Flood (or) Isolation	
		—"All talk, no listen"	—"Keep yourselves unspotted from the world." —cloister

life are sadly in error and hardly worthy of notice, let alone respect or credence.[1]

Not only is theirs the only interpretation, but it explains everything. No significant areas of ignorance, ambiguity, or questioning are admitted, and certainly no error. It is a closed system, perfect and complete, sufficient for all purposes, needing no revision and permitting none. It is usually promulgated by a charismatic founder or prophet (Menno Simons, John Wesley, Joseph Smith, George Fox, Charles T. Russell and "Judge" Rutherford, Elijah Muhammed, etc.) as the authoritative teaching of Truth for all time, and becomes the unchanging standard to which all followers must adhere with uncritical and unreflective tenacity. (Of course, such systems *do* change as shifting times require, even as Mormonism changed with the introduction of polygamy in 1852 and its subsequent abandonment in 1890, but these revisions are seldom acknowledged as such; they are "new dispensations" perfecting the old, or—to use a Roman Catholic phrase—"development of doctrine" that was already implicit in the original revelation.) At its worst, such absolutism leads the faithful to hatred and persecution

1. Cf. Elmer T. Clark, *The Small Sects in America* (New York: Abingdon Press, 1949), in which, time after time, the following type of statement appears: "[This body] does not regard itself as a denomination but as a movement within the church universal to restore Christian unity on a Scriptural basis" (p. 80). "This sect, like others, not only feels that it is not a sect, but is actually out to rid the world of sects" (p. 111).

of competing truths and their adherents; at best, they are simply not interested in what, in their view, can only be error.

5. *Conformity.* If the members of a religious group willingly accept a rigorous discipline, obey their leaders unquestioningly, and suffer punishment without abandoning the group, they also require of one another a fairly strict conformity, not only in matters of faith and morals but in life-style (or rather, faith and morals for them include many details of dress, demeanor, and expression that outsiders would consider peripheral to religion and properly subjects of individual choice). Deviance and dissent are not indulged. Those who depart from the strait and narrow—even in seemingly innocuous ways—are soon corrected, often by their peers rather than by their leaders, through such devices as group confessions, mutual criticisms (Oneida Community), "shunning," suspension, excommunication, or more vigorous measures (the Danite Band of the Mormons?).

A much misunderstood feature of such groups is their peculiarity of dress or speech or conduct—some eccentric traits that single them out from the rest of the population, often for ridicule, obloquy, discrimination, persecution. Why do the Amish or the Hasidim persist in wearing their peculiar garb, which often inspires "outside" bullies to torment the children of the group? These peculiarities are the uniform of the group, which demonstrates to all that they are different from other people. These are their shared stigmata of solidarity, their badge of belonging. The ridicule and persecution it draws down, even upon children, is an important element in reinforcing the mutual support within the group and in increasing their separation from the hostile outside world. They often display their strange uniform with pride and in full expectation of persecution. In fact, the latter is often welcomed, if not courted, as an opportunity for demonstrating their fidelity to the faith, their willingness to suffer for it. It becomes a source of merit even unto martyrdom. This does not justify their harassment, but suggests that even persecution may redound to the reinforcement of social strength by increasing the cost of belonging, heightening the demand upon members, raising the validation of the meanings carried by the group.

6. *Fanaticism.* If the members of a religious group are filled with missionary zeal to tell others the Good News of the meanings they have found and refuse to be silenced even at the price of suffering or death, it also seems to be the case that the members of such a group show a corresponding trait which might be called fanaticism, in the specific sense that their communications are predominantly outgoing. That is, outflow exceeds inflow because of two possible mechanisms: either a flood of outgoing messages that swamps any incoming ones, or an isolation, a cloister, into which messages from the outside world are unable to penetrate. For the outsider who has his own religious views, which he feels are entitled to some consideration and respect, it is disillusioning to discover that the fanatic is not really interested in what he has to say. There is no genuine give-and-take of discussion; at best it is a disputation, in which his views are given only the attention needed to refute them. He feels (correctly) that he is not getting through to the other party, who is "all talk and no listen." He has only two choices: to capitulate (concede, accept, convert) or to withdraw from the conversation (if he can).[2]

Traits of Leniency

These three traits of strictness which I have called absolutism, conformity, and fanaticism make the religious movements described rather uncomfortable to live with. Why can they not be more reasonable—respectable—reciprocal? Since we are constructing a model of what a strong religion might be, suppose we substitute for these distressing features a set of more amiable ones which we might characterize inclusively as "leniency." If we are designing an ideal type, why not make it really ideal?

Describing leniency in the three dimensions used earlier, we would have the traits seen in Chart C.

2. Intriguing hypotheses for empirical research in the area of communications are suggested by this formulation, such as: the greater the dominance of outgoing messages over incoming, the greater will be the accession of members; or (conversely) the greater the dominance of incoming messages over outgoing, the greater will be the loss of members.

CHART C: TRAITS OF LENIENCY

GOALS	CONTROLS	COMMUNICATION
7. *Relativism* —belief that no one has a monopoly on truth; that all insights are partial —attachment to many values and to various modes of fulfilment (not just the religious) —a critical and circumspect outlook	8. *Diversity* —appreciation of individual differences (everyone should "do his thing") —no heresy trials; no excommunications; no humiliating group confessions of error —leadership is institutionalized, not charismatic	9. *Dialogue* —an exchange of differing insights, an exploration of divergent views —appreciative of outsiders rather than judgmental (inflow > outflow)

7. *Relativism.* An organization designed to work in harmony with its neighbors and the spirit of the times would recognize that no one has a monopoly on truth. All insights are partial, and, dispersed among many persons and organizations, they serve as correctives to one another. A religious body of this type would also recognize that there are various modes of fulfillment in addition to the religious. People have many interests and values that are important, and religion cannot expect to monopolize all their talents or attention. Moreover, the modern person is properly skeptical of sweeping claims to truth asserted by anyone, and he tends to resist domination by the pretensions of any organization.

8. *Diversity.* In the modern, reasonable organization, there should be an appreciation of the richness of individual differences. Each person has something unique to contribute to the common experience if he is encouraged and enabled to develop it. Let a thousand flowers bloom! Everyone should "do his own thing" when he "gets it together." Certainly in such an association there would be no unseemly heresy trials, with some members sitting in judgment on others, the former excommunicating the latter for some imputed ideological taint or deficiency. If there are internal difficulties in the society, it should be possible for mature human beings to work them out without resort to humiliating confessions, penances, or abjections.

9. *Dialogue.* No organization can claim to be part of the contemporary world that doesn't understand and engage in dialogue—the exchange of differing insights among equals, the exploration of

divergent or contrasting heritages or viewpoints by courteous urbane discussants, able to present their own beliefs irenically and to appreciate the strengths of others' beliefs. The truly mature person (or group) has nothing to fear from listening to others; if anything, it deepens his understanding of his own heritage and convictions. The encounter with outsiders need not be a life-or-death struggle against an enemy who will upset one's hard-won faith if his cannot be upset first. It need not be a debate, which must be "won" or "lost." Rather it can be a cooperative exploration of common problems for the mutual enlightenment of all.

Who would not rather belong to, work with, live near a group of this kind than one with the traits of strictness? More and more people seem to feel this way, as we see great religious organizations becoming more ecumenical, willing to recognize others' claims to existence, integrity, validity. Even formerly exclusivist groups are beginning cautiously to let down their guard and risk reciprocal relationships. Why not strive for a *strong ecumenical* organization (Charts A and C) and have the best of both worlds?

Evidences of Social Weakness

The main hypothesis of this book is that *social strength and leniency do not seem to go together*. In groups showing traits of leniency, the concomitant is not social strength but weakness— Row D of Chart D, where we now see the four rows of our model in perspective.

10. *Lukewarmness*. It is only human to feel that "if you have some truth and I have some truth, why should either of us die for his portion?" That is the reasonable approach. Surely between even the most seemingly irreconcilable opposites there can be found a formulation that will be mutually acceptable. The balanced, mature person with an awareness of the wide range of values and interests open to modern man is not going to sacrifice all (or much) for any single set of values or any sole area of fulfillment. Rather he will try to find an equilibrium among them, to compensate for

CHART D: "STRONG" AND "WEAK" GROUPS

Social Dimensions		GOALS	CONTROLS	COMMUNICATION
"STRONG" GROUPS	A — Evidences of Social Strength	1. *Commitment* —willingness to sacrifice status, possessions, safety, life itself, for the cause or the company of the faithful —a total response to a total demand —group solidarity —total identification of individual's goals with group's	2. *Discipline* —willingness to obey the commands of (charismatic) leadership without question —willingness to suffer sanctions for infraction rather than leave the group	3. *Missionary Zeal* —eagerness to tell the "good news" of one's experience of salvation to others —refusal to be silenced (Acts 5:26) —internal communications stylized and highly symbolic: a cryptic language —winsomeness
	B — Traits of Strictness	4. *Absolutism* —belief that "we have the Truth and all others are in error" —closed system of meaning and value which explains everything —uncritical and unreflective attachment to a single set of values	5. *Conformity* —intolerance of deviance or dissent —shunning of outcasts (*Meidung*) —shared stigmata of belonging (Quaker garb and plain talk) —group confessions or criticisms (Oneida) —separatism	6. *Fanaticism* (outflow > inflow) Flood (or) Isolation —"All talk, no listen" / —"Keep yourselves unspotted from the world" —cloister
"WEAK" GROUPS	C — Traits of Leniency	7. *Relativism* —belief that no one has a monopoly on truth; that all insights are partial —attachment to many values and to various modes of fulfillment (not just the religious) —a critical and circumspect outlook	8. *Diversity* —appreciation of individual differences (everyone should "do his thing") —no heresy trials; no excommunications; no humiliating group confessions of error —leadership is institutionalized, not charismatic	9. *Dialogue* —an exchange of differing insights, an exploration of divergent views —appreciative of outsiders rather than judgmental (inflow > outflow)
	D — Evidences of Social Weakness	10. *Lukewarmness* —"If you have some truth and I have some truth, why should either of us die for his portion?" —reluctance to sacrifice all for any single set of values or area of fulfillment —indecisiveness even when important values are at stake	11. *Individualism* —unwillingness to give unquestioning obedience to anyone —individuality prized above conformity —discipline? for what? —leave group rather than be inconvenienced by its demands	12. *Reserve* —reluctance to expose one's personal beliefs or to impose them on others —consequent decay of the missionary enterprise —no effective sharing of conviction or spiritual insight within the group

losses in one sector of his life by maximizing satisfactions elsewhere. He will recognize the validity of conflicting views, the complexity of countervailing forces, although this may conduce to in-
decisiveness when a choice must be made between alternatives that
cannot be combined or reconciled. He will be a balancer, a tem-
porizer, an equivocator, and organizations composed of his ilk
will be correspondingly ambivalent and immobilized.[3]

11. *Individualism.* The appreciation of individual worth and
freedom is one of the highest achievements of modern man, but it
does not do much for social strength. If each member is unwilling
to give unquestioning obedience (or even much questioning obedience) to a leader or group, it makes for an atomistic aggregation
of individualists rather than a cohesive, deployable organization.
As individuality becomes prized above conformity, discipline ceases
to be binding. It works only until it comes in conflict with each
individual's convictions, disposition, or convenience, whereupon he
is inclined to abandon the group rather than submit to its demands.
Certainly he is willing to cooperate with any reasonable discipline
(if it isn't called that), but he wants to know why, to what end he
is cooperating, what necessitates a particular action or restraint.
(This is precisely the problem confronting the U.S. Army as it
attempts to be more lenient toward individualism while preserving
the essentials of discipline.)

12. *Reserve.* One of the by-products of individualism seems to
be a reluctance to expose one's personal convictions and deepest
feelings to public scrutiny, let alone to flaunt or intrude or impose
them unsought on indifferent or resistant others. One would think
that the atmosphere of dialogue would diminish this privatism,
and it does in certain special circumstances: among receptive peers
in a climate of mutual encouragement. But that is a far cry from
missionary zeal; no strong religious movement ever got far on a

3. ". . . if values are relative and everyone acknowledges the strong possibility that he may be wrong, then no value assumes an emotionally compelling quality. . . . Such cultural relativity of values leads to the elimination of
whole-hearted value involvement and inevitable . . . lassitude." Morris Rosen-
berg, "The Meaning of Politics in Mass Society," *Public Opinion Quarterly*
v. 15, p. 11.

diffident, believe-and-let-believe approach—it spells the decay of any very effective missionary outreach. Furthermore, such reserve leads to the atrophy of any sharing of conviction or spiritual insight within the group. Whereas our fathers used to be able to ask and answer the question "How are things with your soul?" and welcomed it as a cue to discuss their spiritual condition, the average member of a religious organization today would not only have difficulty understanding it and wonder how to reply, but might well be overcome with embarrassment.

To reiterate the main hypothesis: *A group with evidences of social strength will proportionately show traits of strictness; a group with traits of leniency will proportionately show evidences of social weakness rather than strength.* This idea is repugnant to some people, who insist that "lenient" organizations can also be "strong." Perhaps they can. No one would be happier than the author to see the hypothesis disproved, but it will take more than insistence to disprove it. For it provides an explanation (perhaps not perfect; perhaps not the only one) for the decline of ecumenical religious societies and the continuing vitality of nonecumenical bodies in the country at this time. At least it provides a better one than the opposite view, which does not explain anything but merely sets forth unsubstantiated suppositions.

For twenty years I have been looking for one clear case that would disprove this theory, but I have not as yet found one. Others may be more successful (or perhaps more objective). At one time I thought the Quakers might qualify, for some of them show strong commitment, discipline, and zeal combined with respect for diversity, dialogue, and a degree of relativism. It is not clear on closer inspection, however, whether these qualities are characteristic of the Quaker fellowship as a whole. To some extent they do seem to be carried by the Quaker tradition (though they were certainly *not* true of George Fox and his immediate followers) and are manifested by a few individuals and small groups. Average Quakers, however, seem to be more like President Nixon than John Woolman, A. J. Muste, or Douglas Steere. That is, they are not caught up in a dynamic movement that shakes them loose from conventional culture, sends them forth in disciplined mission, at great sacrifice, for the sake of meaning. With the exception of outstanding individuals and a few small cells, Friends seem more like members of typical ecumenical religious organizations than like any of the four movements described in the preceding chapters. This is only an impression, however, gathered from many varied but scattered contacts with Quakers. A more thorough and systematic study might justify a different conclusion.

The Ecumenical Gradient

It is not an easy hypothesis to prove or disprove until it can be quantified in some meaningful way. Observable evidences of social strength (such as membership growth, per capita giving, sanctions assigned and accepted, missionaries dispatched, and so on) would have to be correlated with indices of strictness/leniency which would be difficult to quantify. Perhaps a crude comparison can be seen in the following effort to arrange denominations and religious bodies in rank-order of ecumenicity.

Suppose one were to list the major religious groups in the United States and then ask each group such questions as these:

Are there any groups on this list

                                                        No.

1. Which your own group does not recognize as
   a. A religious organization?   _____
   b. A Christian church?   _____
2. With which your own group would not officially
   cooperate or engage in joint activities?   _____
3. Whose baptism, or other basic entrance rites, you
   do not recognize as valid?   _____
4. With whom you do not share communion, or other
   comparable selective rite or sacrament?   _____
5. With whom you do not encourage intermarriage?   _____

6. With whom, your group would *not* transfer members on a basis of parity (equal recognition by both groups) and without the preparation that would be given a neophyte?   _____

7. With whom you would not exchange clergy or pulpits?   _____

Without having asked such questions or received replies, we may imagine that there are some religious groups whose answers to all or most of the questions would be in very low numbers, if not a series of zeros. There are conceivably others whose answers to each question would be the total number of groups on the list minus one (their own). If we were to arrange the groups from top to bottom in descending order of aggregate score from maximum to minimum, we might see something like Chart E.

The empirical rank-order of exclusivism might not be exactly that suggested here; the Episcopal Church might score higher than the Reformed Church rather than lower (this could be the result of questions triggering the apostolic-succession response of the former more often than a comparable form of exclusiveness in the latter). But anyone familiar with religious life in America today would have little doubt that the United Church of Christ would score lower than the Lutheran churches, or that the Southern Baptist Convention would score higher than the American Baptist Convention, or that the Jehovah's Witnesses, Mormons, Seventh-day Adventists, and Orthodox Jews would be at the opposite end of the continuum from Unitarians, Ethical Culture, and Reform Jews.

The fine scaling in between will have to await empirical testing. The questions on which such ranking is based are designed to elicit indications of strictness which are (*a*) conscious, (*b*) admissible, and (*c*) commensurate. That is, groups are usually quite aware of their views and actions with respect to the acceptability of other groups of the same kind. It is part of the development of identity, of boundary definition. Moreover, it is something that can be candidly asserted (if anything is; some of the groups highest on the

CHART E: THE EXCLUSIVIST–ECUMENICAL GRADIENT

(Black Muslims*)
Jehovah's Witnesses
Evangelicals and Pentecostals
(Orthodox Jews*)
Churches of Christ
Latter-day Saints (Mormons)
Seventh-day Adventists
Church of God
Church of Christ, Scientist
Southern Baptist Convention
Lutheran Church–Missouri Synod
American Lutheran Church
Roman Catholic Church
(Conservative Jews*)
Russian Orthodox
Greek Orthodox
Lutheran Church in America
Southern Presbyterian Church
Reformed Church in America
Episcopal Church
American Baptist Convention
United Presbyterian Church
United Methodist Church
United Church of Christ
(Reform Jews*)
Ethical Culture Society
Unitarian-Universalists

scale would probably refuse to answer any questions put to them by outsiders, as was the experience of Stroup with Jehovah's Witnesses). Few bodies are likely to reveal the number of members excommunicated during the previous year, or to expose the grounds (if any) for lesser sanctions. And as between groups, which sanctions, short of exclusion, would be equivalent? Would the measurement of outflow/inflow of messages for one group be applicable to

* Jewish groups should occupy a separate continuum, as should Islamic groups. They are inserted here to show where they might fall on a composite gradient.

another? In addition to being conscious, admissible, and commensurate, the quality or cluster of qualities evoked by the questions on exclusiveness/ecumenicity are believed to indicate or represent the whole syndrome of strictness—though they do not exhaust it.

We are supposing that there is a quality or cluster of qualities by which religious bodies can be ranked on a continuum from exclusiveness to ecumenicity, and that certain bodies will be ranked high by virtually all knowledgeable observers while others will be ranked low. This much may be conceded more readily than the other half of the hypothesis, which is that religious organizations with a low score on the exclusiveness scale *will also be less vigorous, less resilient, less growing than those with a high one.* To put it in its grossest, most simplistic form: other things being equal, *bodies low on the list will tend to diminish in numbers while those high on the list will tend to increase.*

The Ecumenical Hurdle

Somewhere in the middle of the scale there is a cutting point which might be labeled the ecumenical hurdle. It is the point above which membership is increasing and below which membership is diminishing. The *rate* of increase or decrease is subject to many and varied factors, and there may be temporary reversals as a result of secular trends, but sooner or later (the hypothesis holds) the relaxations of social weakness will become apparent in shrinking membership and other ways. In earlier chapters it was noted that some denominations are declining; these are also those low on the exclusiveness scale. Others are growing at various rates; these are also high on the exclusiveness scale.

It is significant that some groups just above the hurdle (the Southern Baptist Convention, the Missouri Synod Lutheran Church) are leveling off; that is, they are increasing in membership at a diminishing rate. Other groups, just below the hurdle (Lutheran Church in America, Southern Presbyterian), have been increasing until very recently and have only begun to decline slightly in the past year or two. Again, the Roman Catholic Church is of special interest. Only a few years ago it would have shown a much higher score on the exclusiveness/ecumenicity questions than it does now. It has also just begun to suffer losses of clergy and membership. It may have succeeded at last in leaping over the ecumenical hurdle!

Some may wonder—if the causes of social weakness have been operating for decades—why they have become visible in membership losses only in the past two or three years. The answer would seem to be that the potential feebleness of the churches has been masked until very recently by the secular trend of religiosity. This would mean a condition affecting the time-series involved which is extraneous to the causal relationship being recorded: in the present case, the expectation that people will attend churches and support religion. This general social expectation has disappeared during recent decades. Once it no longer regularized and confirmed religious custom, many people whose churchgoing had been an unreflective cultural conformity began to ask themselves whether they were getting enough out of it to be worth the bother. And with that thought, the accumulated ennui of years caught up with them, the religious boom collapsed, and the growth curves began to fall back to earth again.

Another reason for the rather precipitate decline of the mainline Protestant churches in the United States at this particular time may be the triggering effect of the sudden discrediting of the formerly "unshakable" Roman Catholic Church. At least one great church was deemed to know its business, even if others didn't; now it too was seen to falter, waver, and stumble. With it fell many lesser churches.

Why Do People Join Churches?

George LaNoue accounts for the great difference in growth rates between liberal and conservative denominations by use of an "incentive" model derived from the work by James G. March and Herbert A. Simon, *Organizations*.[4] In this model, an organization

4. New York: John Wiley & Sons, 1958. LaNoue's work is not in published form.

is characterized by the incentives which it offers its members to give time, effort, and money to its activities. Every organization offers a menu of various incentives—recognition, compensation, sundry services and emoluments, comradeship, recreation, acquisition of skills or expertise, etc.—and members tacitly choose among them. LaNoue observes that liberal churches have increasingly sought to develop an array of inducements that would appeal to the widest range of potential members, yet with diminishing emphasis upon the one incentive unique to churches, that given preeminence by conservative churches: salvation (which he tends to identify with a promise of supernatural life after death).

Since the incentives held out by the liberal churches—fellowship, entertainment, knowledge (about personality and adjustment, planned parenthood, woman's liberation, home management, and so on), respectability, etc.—are offered by many other (non-religious) groups, those churches place themselves in competition for adherents with organizations which may have more compelling forms of the same attractions. An example LaNoue gives is civil rights: persons wanting to work for civil rights will find a more specialized and effective vehicle in the NAACP or the Urban League or other groups devoted to that cause than in even the most activist churches. If that is the incentive that satisfies them, they may be drawn to churches which are engaged in that sort of activity. But if and when the church turns its attention to another issue, they will readily abandon it for an organization that still pursues civil rights.

Conservative churches, on the other hand, offer an incentive (or commodity?) that is not as widely available—salvation—and offer it persistently. Thus they are spared competition from more highly specialized secular organizations; their only competition is from other conservative churches, which is more limited and easier to handle (they are fighting on their own turf, as it were). Persons forced to limit their nonoccupational interests, activities, and expenditures will tend to eliminate those that are marginal in favor of those whose incentives are intensive and unique.

LaNoue adds a further dimension by referring to the population(s) of potential members from which these two types of churches seek to draw. He maintains that the population "pool" susceptible to the characteristic appeals of conservative churches is shrinking, whereas that (supposedly) open to the typical appeals of liberal churches is growing. Thus the conservative churches have been highly successful in enlisting, and perhaps have nearly exhausted, their potential membership; while the liberal churches have been even less successful in attracting their potential membership (although this is increasing) than their proportion of members among the general population might suggest.

Though developed independently and phrased somewhat differently, LaNoue's theory is very similar to the one advanced here. His characterization of the conservative incentive as salvation, equating it with a supernatural assurance of life after death, is a narrower (perhaps *too* narrow) concept of what religion distinctively does for men. It is probably true that conservative churches in the United States are seen, and see themselves, offering salvation in the form of supernatural immortality, but that is not the only form salvation takes, even within Christianity. It is only one way of answering the basic questions of ultimate meaning, and one which has not been characteristic of several great religions (Judaism, Confucianism, Buddhism).

In this narrow sense, LaNoue is probably correct when he says that conservative churches are appealing to an ever-diminishing reservoir of older, rural and small-town people who are responsive to traditional assurances of supernatural salvation. If religion is confined to persons who are culturally conditioned to seek and accept that particular formulation of ultimate meaning, then its prospects are indeed dwindling. And it cannot be denied that there is an important dimension of what Peter Berger calls intellectual plausibility as well as cultural acceptability that determines the appeal of a particular religion for most people in a given time and place. But, as indicated earlier, a really vigorous religious movement *is not hindered by an inhospitable cultural climate—it makes its own plausibility-structure*[5] and (all too soon) acquires

5. Peter Berger's term in *The Sacred Canopy.*

acceptance. It does so, not by appealing to most people, but by attracting a rather limited number of persons who will respond to its high demand, binding them into an intense, disciplined, and zealous movement and sweeping over every obstacle to exercise an inspiring influence in most men's lives—even those who originally would have found it implausible or unacceptable.

But, LaNoue (or someone else) might say, that's precisely what's gone out of style! The number of people who are inclined to respond to a high-demand movement of *any* kind is dwindling and soon will disappear. In the future, religion will be a much more dispersed and reflective sort of activity, linked not by organized collective rites but by electronic media (such as the eternal chant of the transistor radio rock music which follows the young wherever they go?) And so it may be. There are elements in man's immediate future which no one has lived before, so who can foretell their effect?

But, as we saw in Chapters II and III, one of the oldest and broadest and deepest continuities in human behavior is that called religion, and it will probably continue as long as there is anything that could be called humanity. Which functions, traits, and forms are essential to such behavior and which are merely culturally conditioned is a debate that has long exercised anthropologists. This book, however, is predicated on the assumption that the dynamic evidenced in the Anabaptist movement, the Wesleyan revival, the Mormon migration, Jehovah's Witnesses, the Black Muslims, and so forth is something deeper than a temporary culture pattern that may go out of style. It is to some important degree a characteristic posture of the human being—the way he discovers, shares, embodies, imparts, lives out, and dies for the ultimate meanings that make sense of his life.

Strong Groups Weaken

Membership increase is not the only index of social strength, by any means. There are corroborative qualities as well, such as those described in Chapter IV, which would be apparent in any Saving

Remnant, whatever its numbers. It would visibly be going some-where, its members obviously devoted to their cause, strengthened rather than discouraged by hardship or persecution, missing no opportunity to tell the glad tidings of their Truth. Given these qualities (according to our hypothesis), the Saving Remnant is going to *grow*, sooner or later, slower or faster; it is going to attract adherents as honey does flies, whether it welcomes them or not. In fact, the more uninviting its aspect, the more they will want to join.

But how can that be, if people are repelled by traits of strictness?

People in general may be repelled, but there are a few—perhaps one in a hundred or one in a thousand—who hunger and thirst after what only the Saving Remnant has to offer, and by the acces-sion of these few it will grow. In this respect it is clearly distinguish-able from the ordinary remnant, which is not saving anyone, not going anywhere, and not growing—either fast or slow—but just hanging on grimly to what is left after the less tenacious and more dissatisfied have departed.

To recapitulate: membership gain or loss is significant over time; what that significance may be is subject to interpretation. The explanation offered here is that (barring extenuating circum-stances) *strong organizations tend to increase in membership and weak ones to diminish*. Thus membership gain or loss is used as a useful, though not sole or infallible, indicator of social strength (as defined in Chapter V). We have also used the exclusiveness/ ecumenicity scale as a composite index of strictness, though by no means the only possible index or a comprehensive one. Now perhaps we are ready for the next step.

We have been thinking of social strength and strictness as static pigeon holes into which organizations may be classified. But they may be thought of in dynamic terms as well: as qualities which affect the evolution of organizations. The static form of our hypothesis, in abbreviated form, is: *strong organizations are strict*. Looking at the specimens in their respective boxes, we may reach a comparative form of the theory: *the stricter, the stronger*—within limits. (That is, there may be a point of diminishing returns beyond which increasing strictness does not produce significantly greater strength, and might in fact prove counterproductive. For instance, an excessively harsh purging of deviants—such as the Inquisition —may result in paralysis of all other activity in the organization.)

This, in turn, suggests the dynamic form: a *strong organization which loses its strictness will also lose its strength.* But the relationship is not only dynamic, it is degenerative, "tilted": *strictness tends to deteriorate into leniency, which results in social weakness in place of strength.*

Why should it be degenerative? Like all energy systems, social organizations are entropic—they gradually run down—they are subsiding toward a state of rest. One has only to reflect upon the strenuous character of the strong organizations described earlier to realize which side of the chart is closer to a state of rest. Another way to put it is that *traits of strictness are harder to maintain in an organization than traits of leniency.* By harder is meant that they require more energy—more determination, more persistence, more effort, more mobilization, etc. If this is indeed the case, then the ecumenical gradient is an arrow pointing from top to bottom. Religious organizations decline and weaken; can they ever become strong again? Is not our gradient a one-way street, running downhill all the way? We shall consider the mechanisms of this process in the next chapter.

Chapter VII

Dynamics of Diminishing Demand

In the preceding material, we have considered the qualities of social strength in religious organizations, as contrasted with qualities of social weakness. We have found traits of strictness associated with social strength and traits of leniency associated with social weakness, and we have wondered whether some sort of causal relationship exists between strength and strictness, and between weakness and leniency, or whether the first in each case simply deteriorates into the second in the course of time. Even if we conclude that entropy tugs at us all, we have not yet explained why its dead weight is a greater drag on some organizations than on others. And there may be those—despite our lengthy scanning of four "strong" religious movements—who do not see what bearing social strength or strictness could have on contemporary religious problems.

Others may have leaped to the wishful or fearful conclusion that churches decline *because* they are ecumenical. This is no more true than that they become ecumenical *because* they are declining. So far as we have seen, neither is the cause of the other, but both are symptoms of an underlying process or condition which makes for diminishing effectiveness in gaining and retaining members, while it also, more or less independently, creates a receptiveness to possibilities of cooperation with other groups of similar kind and common objectives. That underlying cause is the entropic or aging process first identified in Wesley's "Law" of the decay of pure religion and later described in rather static terms by Ernst Troeltsch in his typology of sect and church.[1]

Why Not a Simpler Explanation?

Still others may wonder why such an elaborate hypothesis is necessary to explain a decline which seems well accounted for by a simpler explanation. Some might contend, for instance, that the mainline churches are declining because they have quit saving souls and have gone in for social action. A second group might maintain that the real cause is the growing secularism of the major churches and their consequent neglect of spiritual concerns. A third faction might hold that the increasing dominance of the clergy in these churches, subordinating the laity to passive roles, is the true reason.

These several simple and sweeping explanations are overlapping, imprecise, and partially true—therefore also partially false. Resentment against radical social activism has probably contributed to the decline of the churches in some quarters, but enthusiasm for securing social justice has increased their attractiveness in others. The explanation is differential: the same phenomenon (social activism) produces at least two, opposite effects with respect to the organizational vigor of churches: it alienates one population and attracts another. The former happens to be the older, entrenched pillars or proprietors of the existing church membership, at least in many instances. Whether it is normal or necessary for corporate bodies, especially religious bodies, to be thus attached to the status quo and resentful of change is a subject for further discussion (see Chapter IX). The question turns on broader axes

1. *The Social Teaching of the Christian Churches* (New York: Harper & Row, 1960; first published, 1911). This has been criticized because it does not provide for the denomination or the cult, etc. Viewed as a limited number of "boxes," it may be an inadequate typology. Viewed as stages in a process of organizational evolution, which may differ from one culture to another, it is as much a step toward fuller knowledge as the classification of stars by color and luminosity was a step toward fitting them on the dynamic evolutionary curve of the "main sequence."

than those apparent in the original simple explanation of the churches' decline.

Furthermore, we cannot discover *which* of the simple explanations is correct without a fuller understanding of what is happening. If secularization is the cause, it has been going on in the churches, in various forms, for decades, if not centuries; why is the decline becoming suddenly obvious just now? The same is true of professionalization and bureaucratization of the clergy: it has been going on since the year One—or at least since 1901. From that time on, there has been a certain ebb and flow of vitality in the churches, usually related to wars and depressions, but no such precipitous and general decline as now seems to be occurring.

Each of these particularistic answers touches on part of the problem besetting the churches, but in just such ways as the several blind men touched different parts of the elephant and thought it each a different kind of beast. Our puzzle is to try to assess what is true and what is false in each simple explanation and—perhaps even more pressing for the pragmatists among us—what, if anything, can be done about it. For these further tasks we need a fuller understanding of what is going on: how organizations operate, what weakens and what strengthens them, what kinds of members they attract, and how. The charts and hypotheses in earlier chapters were designed to help us understand what is going on, at least in broad outline. But the texture of verisimilitude may not be present until we can grapple further with some of the specific mechanisms by which organizations grow and decay.

Who Responds to a High Demand?

We have noted that the strong religious organization makes very high demands upon its members. They must give it absolute and unswerving allegiance; be willing to work, suffer, and die for it; abandon all competing activities, allegiances, and responsibilities in its favor; tell its Good News tirelessly and unselfconsciously to strangers; wear its stigmata of humiliation on their bodies; submit to its strictures, conformities, and disciplines; go where they are sent and do what they are told. Not everyone responds favorably to such demands, some are in fact repelled by them. What are the causes and consequences of this differential appeal?

Max Weber in his *Sociology of Religion* refers to those who are willing to give religious interests such an exceptional proportion of their energies as "virtuosi of religion." Apparently he felt that some people will excell at that sort of thing and others won't. He did not attempt to explain why some are virtuosi and others not, since that would have led him astray into individual rather than collective traits, and he was writing a sociology rather than a psychology of religion.

Eric Hoffer has suggested that the "true believer"—the candidate for fanatical (high-demand) religious movements—is the person who, for one reason or another, feels that his life is "irremediably spoiled" and therefore clings obsessively to a movement that can supply significance and purpose for his life which it lacks in itself. He lists several categories of such persons: the poor, the bored, misfits, minorities, sinners, etc. That is, there are several kinds of conditions which can lead or drive individuals to sacrifice themselves to a source of significance outside themselves because they feel they have lost all significance within.

It is neither necessary nor appropriate here to evaluate the *psychological* soundness of Hoffer's diagnosis. Although sweepingly aphoristic, it is a magnificent contribution to the *sociology* of mass movements. As another effort to make a sociological contribution, this work cannot try to determine the psychological motivations of individuals—whether they seek significance in total allegiance to a high-demand movement solely because they feel they have no significance within themselves. For our purposes we can disregard the final clause—let those affirm it who prefer—and simply say there are many kinds of conditions which can lead or drive individuals to sacrifice themselves to a source of significance outside themselves. Thus we do not prejudge or denigrate any of them. The fact remains that there are such people; what their motivations may be we need not now determine. History and experience suggest that they are not numerous: those persons who, for whatever reason, are potentially receptive to high-demand movements. Perhaps one in a hundred or one in a thousand. For the interest and allegiance of these few, the movements of a given hour compete.

There is a venerable Christian theological dispute about the ancient statement that "many are called, but few are chosen." Are there only a few elect or elite virtuosi who will respond to a high-demand to serve the cause of meaning? As a descendant of the Arminian rather than the Calvinist wing of this division, I hold that *all* men are potential responders to the call—that all men *want* to be called and want to answer—more than anything else in the world, since for this they were made. But only a few actually do hear the call and make a total response, so perhaps it comes to the same thing in the end.

Not all persons will be receptive to the same appeal; not all will be willing or able to respond to the same degree. We may suppose that *the higher the demand a movement makes on its followers, the fewer there will be who respond to it, but the greater the individual and aggregate impact of those who do respond.* One measure of demand is the degree of disruption of a person's former thoughts, habits, relationships, and life-style that it requires. Another is the scope of the believer's continuing attitudes, activities, and interests that it commandeers: that is, vocational, familial, recreational, artistic, etc. Most high-demand movements are relatively totalitarian in this respect—they want to dominate every aspect of their members' lives. A quantitative value of that domination would be a third measure of demand: how much of the believer's time, and income (or income-producing capacity) does the movement utilize? Again, the high-demand movement will, by the urgency of its endeavor, seek to monopolize its member's every waking hour—and will frequently succeed!

As suggested in Chapter IV, any organization that can enlist virtually all the time and energy of its members—even though they be few in number and limited in ability—in a single-minded, meaning-motivated venture has harnessed an engine that is in a category of magnitude as much beyond our ordinary vehicles of collective effort as the jet plane is beyond the horse-drawn carriage. Such an organization has no reason to be overawed by the exalted executive suites of Wall Street or Madison Avenue. When the members of one such group were astonished at the towering buildings of the big city, their leader reminded them of the true measure of things in human life with the words, "there will not be left here one stone upon another. . . ." (Matt. 24:2).

Some will leave father and mother, spouse and children, livelihood and possessions, to serve the cause. Some may have been but waiting for an imperious summons to call them away from onerous responsibilities or monotonous routine which they were all too ready to leave. Others may have found it a genuinely rending but redeeming wrench away from trivialities and earthly treasures. Out of better or baser motives they come, and in the intensity of the high-demand movement are transformed into selfless emissaries of ultimate meaning. Some in time may become disillusioned for one reason or another and fall away, but whatever their motivation and whatever its duration, members of the high-demand movement are lifted by it into a zone of focused devotion, intense activity, and shared struggle that means more to them, while they are in it, than life itself.

What Slows the Movement?

By its very ardor, that zone creates a boundary turbulence between itself and the calmer regions of the world. Its abrasiveness supplies part of the friction that slows it down. On every side, hands reach out to grasp it, buffet it, or cling to it, and each imparts its perturbation. For instance, when the group gets large enough to need a meeting place bigger and more permanent than someone's livingroom, it begins to impinge upon the force fields of territoriality. Most of the real estate on this crowded planet is already staked out, and those who want to use it will have to enter into negotiations with those who staked it. The tabernacle that is more than a tent will have to come to terms with landlords. The Kingdom Hall with a mortage on it will not be quite so quick to identify bankers as part of Satan's organization—at least not when word gets back to the banker. By the giving of such hostages to the powers that be are the most radical of prophetic movements eventually domesticated.

In his recollections of his childhood in the Oneida Community, Pierrepont Noyes describes the forces that finally compelled the Perfectionists (led by his father, John Humphrey Noyes) to abandon their unique system of complex marriage and other communal aspects of their historic experiment and to become a joint-stock company.[2] He recounts the social and economic difficulties encountered by the elders, at least as a child dimly perceived them. But there was nothing dim about his awareness of the taunts and jibes which the town boys directed at his community-made homespun garb. Such attacks at all levels, especially by outraged orthodox Protestant clergymen upon the allegedly depraved free love practiced at Oneida—actually a very sober and puritanical system—at last slowed the movement to a stop in 1880 after only thirty-five years. Today only the relics of the big Community House are left at Kenwood, N.Y., and the eminently respectable silverplate firm in which some of the descendants of the Perfectionists are still employed.

"Pip" Noyes as a boy had difficulty comprehending what the Community his father had founded was all about. His perplexity calls our attention to the main shoal on which most high-demand movements eventually run aground: passing on the faith to the next generation. However charismatic the founder, however devoted his followers, however numerous their adult converts, they will find difficulty in transmitting their ultimate answers to children who are not old enough to ask the questions. Sometimes an immunization takes place through premature encounter with even the most dynamic gospel. The "halfway covenant" in colonial New England was a concession on the part of the Congregational churches to

2. Pierrepont B. Noyes, *My Father's House* (New York: Farrar & Rinehart, 1937).

this lukewarmness in the children of believers and *their* children, who could not meet the demands (of conversion, consciousness of election, and so on) their fathers had met, yet out of filial affection were granted a partial membership. By such accommodations, in each generation a little of the force leaks away until eventually the once dynamic movement is indistinguishable from the environing world.

Similar to the problem of *perpetuation* is that of *propagation*. Franklin H. Littell has frequently noted both in the history of churches in the United States.[3] They not only "halved the covenant" for their children again and again until there was scarcely a sliver left, but also progressively relaxed the standards of membership for those coming in from outside who could make no filial claim. In order to build up mass memberships, they have taken in many new members whose preparation was sketchy at best. Such members often had only the vaguest notion of what the church they were joining believed or required (which often was not a great deal), and perhaps thought it rather similar in general to their own ideas and attitudes, not that it made any difference (and in fact it didn't).

As a result, Littell observes, the churches became filled with baptized pagans, who soon far outnumbered those who had gained and kept some understanding of the obligations of discipleship. The churches then became unable to enforce any such obligations. The newly baptized might have taken umbrage to be told that there are some ways of speaking, thinking, or acting which are not consistent with being a Christian, and that one might have to choose between them. Consequently, for lack of information to the contrary, many church members enjoy the impression that whatever they are accustomed to believe, say, or do is somehow Christian since they are, after all, Christians. The problem of propagation, then, is how to put *content* into *conversion*—to train new members in the distinctive ideas, attitudes, actions, and discipline of the movement. Some churches are better at this than others, but in the best of them there is still a certain amount of slippage.

3. Cf. *The Origins of Sectarian Protestantism* (New York: Macmillan Co., 1964) and *From State Church to Pluralism* (New York: Doubleday, 1962).

The Peril of Success

And even when this is at a minimum, the organization's social strength is not secure. Wesley's Law of the Decay of Pure Religion describes a danger which overtakes even the most zealous movement: *success*. We may grant the purest heart in a convert, concede the most rigorous and effective training, allow no backsliding, hypocrisy, or self-righteousness, and still expect some weakening of zeal and discipline in time, and for the least blameworthy reasons. As men grow older, surmount their difficulties, gather wisdom from experience, and earn the respect of their fellows, the world becomes a broader place, with diverse crafts, virtues, and satisfactions of merit comparable to those found in religion. Important as unfailing fidelity to the faith and unflinching adherence to its discipline may be, they are not the only worthy elements in life. Circumstances may arise in which some of these other qualities compete —if they do not conflict—with them. One can readily think of such conflicts between faith and freedom, for instance, or between faith and justice, faith and beauty, or faith and (empirical) truth. And given the loftier perspective on life which comes with the most modest elevation, it is sometimes possible for a once zealous convert to shade the faith a little for another good. If that is what Wesley meant by "the pride of life," it is a failing which few will be single-minded or faith-dominated enough to avoid.

The same broadening of interests and concerns is apparent in churches as well as in their members. Some churchmen have, for the most commendable of motives, concluded that God desires his servants to seek justice, freedom, beauty, and truth as well as obedient faith. In fact, they may have reached the heretical conclusion that there are obediences more important to God than maintaining the social strength of a particular institution—even His Church! This is a brave and lofty sentiment for a day when institutions are not highly esteemed, but we should not be astonished if it does not prevent the decline of churches.

Strength and Function

Many of the dynamics of social strength described in the preceding pages may well apply to all or most types of organization. Since our focus has been on religious bodies, I have not tried to explore the limits of applicability to other types with which I am less familiar; instead, the possibility of a wider application has been left open for those who may wish to pursue it. In addition, the species of religious organization shades away at the edges, as do many distinctions, into closely related and analogous entities. Hoffer writes of quasi-religious movements such as Communism and Nazism, which are similar to religious movements in their original scope, demand, and recruitment, though different in conceptual content, objectives, mode of operation, or the like. It is not always easy to draw the boundaries of applicability for a particular hypothesis; the somewhat inexact approach used here is to let it run as far as it fits. The writer has tried to focus on the religious scene without feeling obliged to cope with every detail in the penumbra.

The reader may also have wondered from time to time what the connection might be between a socially strong organization and one which is effectively performing its chosen or attributed function(s). Are they supposed to be the same? Or are two independent qualities involved? The answer seems to be somewhere in between, at least regarding the religious function (defined earlier). The effective fulfilling of that function cannot be neatly and exclusively identified with religious organizations possessing social strength. The latter, as we have found, is a trait preeminently characteristic of religious and quasi-religious movements, but it exists also in other organizations which display similar qualities. Likewise, effective religious functioning is inherent in religious movements but extends to other, similar organizations, *in a different direction* so to speak. Perhaps a diagram of the overlapping coverage may clarify this point.

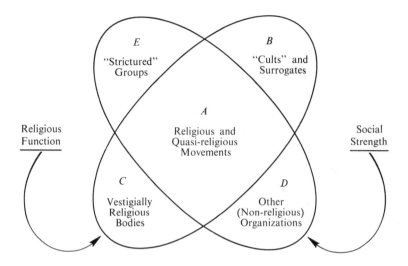

The ellipse beginning at the lower left represents organizations performing the religious function. This is most clearly and squarely involved in area *A*—the religious and quasi-religious movements in the center—and less completely so in the two adjacent regions where it is performed with less effectiveness.

Cults and Surrogates (B). Cults are esoteric teachings which do not aspire to become conventional religious bodies or have not yet succeeded in doing so (such as Unity, Theosophy, Rosicrucianism, Spiritualism, Scientology, etc.); they might be termed invitations to religion which have not as yet been definitively accepted, yet which do explain life at least partially—speculatively or sporadically—to a shifting, dispersed or "sampling" clientele. In this category would also fall organizations that do not claim to be religious, but nevertheless may explain life—i.e., perform the religious function—for some people. To the degree they do so they are functional surrogates for religion. Examples might include philosophies, fraternal orders, community organizations, labor unions, or whatever.

Vestigially Religious Bodies (*C*). These were once in the position of area *A* but have since lost both social strength (which is why they are not in the area of overlap) and much of their religious function, though not all. Their members still derive whatever ultimate meanings they have from the residue deposited in these organizations by earlier, more vigorous generations.

The ellipse that begins at the lower right represents the class of socially strong organizations, centering on religious and quasi-religious movements but including also *D*, other strong but non-religious organizations, and *E*, a somewhat hypothetical category of what could be called "strictured" bodies: that is, those which have attained or retained the quality of social strength without performing any generally recognized function.

Note should be taken of the apparent relationship of social strength to effective functioning. If the foregoing description and generalization are valid, those organizations which are most clearly and effectively fulfilling the religious function for their members are also the organizations that most obviously display social strength, and conversely. It may not be necessary or possible to determine whether they are strong because they are effective or effective because they are strong. Probably both; it would seem likely to be a reciprocal relationship, each factor reinforcing the other. In reverse, those organizations which are *not* effectively fulfilling the religious function would be or become socially weak, and weak organizations would have difficulty in functioning effectively.

Some lodges or fraternal orders might fit into the "strictured" category if their requirements are rigorous enough. All of us have known zealously devoted lodge members whom—so near is meaning to devotion—we have suspected of making the lodge their religion. However, most members of most lodges do not take very seriously the pretentious pseudo-religious rhetoric and ritual and regalia designed to give some semblance of solemnity and purpose to their gatherings; they don't get their explanation of life from it; it isn't their religion. Yet neither do they take with any greater seriousness the organizational demands made upon them; there is little commitment, discipline, or zeal on behalf of the lodge among them; the lodge is not typically an enterprise of distinguished social strength.

There remains the logical possibility, at least, of an organization having great social strength yet which serves no manifest function.[4] It would be distinguished from strong organizations in class *D*, which are presumably serving some important and acknowledged function, though not a religious one. Perhaps Class *E* does not actually have any viable members. The reason it is introduced at this point is to lead us to a significant distinction.

Stringency and Stricture

Earlier we noted traits of strictness in strong organizations; closer examination would suggest that these take two forms, one of which we might call "stringent" and the other "strictured" to indicate the degree of spontaneity involved. In the beginning of a strong religious movement, strictness is not a quality imposed from without so much as arising spontaneously among the adherents. For example, we saw in Chapter VI that in the early stages of the movement nonconformity is often punished by peers rather than by leaders. All the members feel a personal and direct responsibility for preserving the purity or discipline or purpose of the organization; they do not wait for leaders to call attention to infractions or defaults and to pronounce penalties. They do it themselves, often in a loving yet firm way; members will even confess and correct their own errors for the sake of the movement and their own wholehearted participation in it. This is the quality I should like to call stringency.

Later in the history of the organization, these qualities do not arise so spontaneously. They must be more or less deliberately and systematically imposed by the leadership. Members no longer cover their ears to avoid hearing dissident ideas; heresy trials must be instituted to extirpate them (and their holders). Discipline is

4. As distinguished from a latent or unrecognized function; see R. K. Merton, *Social Theory and Social Structure* (Glencoe, Ill.: Free Press, 1949).

imposed by the stern leader upon shamed and sheepish members. Sometimes even the form of confession and self-denunciation is retained (as in Communist trials), but this too is part of the stricture imposed from above to keep the organization in order. In the communications dimension, if a flood of outgoing messages does not spring unbidden from the lips of the faithful, the leadership can provide a substitute in the form of outpourings of printed and broadcast verbiage, or try to cut off the flow of incoming messages from the world by some form of isolation or iron curtain.

Stringency—the spontaneous self-governing strictness of the early movement—all too soon gives way to stricture—the imposed, external imitation of it. Yet even the counterfeit, we may suspect, has sufficed to keep moribund churches tottering along with incredible longevity. This is especially true of some of the oldest Christian traditions: one has only to read of the Coptic and Abyssinian Christians fighting their annual battle for possession of disputed space in the Church of the Holy Sepulchre in Jerusalem to marvel at the tenacity of religious commitments and the prolongation of such tenacity by strictures maintaining absolutism, separatism, fanaticism. The Old Order Amish would be a strictured survival of Anabaptist stringency; Littell refers to it as "somewhat fossilized."

The Roman Catholic Church maintained a monumental social strength for centuries in part by the assiduous preservation of ancient strictures. But at Vatican II the shell was broken, and the strength then dissipated much more rapidly than might have been expected from mere normal decay. This thesis is confirmed by James Hitchcock in his *Decline and Fall of Radical Catholicism*,[5] in which he documents the mild reforms initially urged by "radicals" only to be followed by bolder and more iconoclastic demands, which in turn brought about defections and disillusionments intuitively warned against by conservatives.

Strictures maintained in the most mechanical way may still lend enough semblance of seriousness to keep a religious organization

5. New York: Herder & Herder, 1971. See also his article in *Commonweal* for May 14, 1971, "Aggiornamento Has Failed," accompanied by an editorial which rejects his diagnosis of failure.

going for a long time. But once that seriousness is dispelled by their abandonment, then social strength leaks fast away. Class *E*, then, would represent strong organizations whose strength is entirely attributable to rigorous strictness rather than to any intrinsic function.

Entropy Is the Simplest Explanation

We have been using physical models: strength flowing away like water gushing out of a tapped tank, organizations running down like an unwound clock. There is no harm in borrowing models from familiar fields so long as we recognize that they are oversimplifications for purposes of explanation. But we must take care not to mistake the model for the reality nor to forget the questions the model may mask. For instance, entropy is an obvious process in the physical universe—is it equally applicable in the social world? Must strength always flow *away* and organizations run *down?* How about the possibility that strength grows with exercise, and organizations flourish like the green bay tree? If we can just switch in some good organic models, we may have the problem licked!

The fallacy of organic models is that they disclose only part of the picture: the tree grows only so long as it can get water, sun, and food. Nor, when the whole energy system is taken into account, does it escape the curse of entropy. Moreover, entropy does not have to be explained, whereas its opposite does. We do not need additional factors to account for organizations running down or social strength ebbing away: this is what will happen eventually if nothing prevents. Our fundamental question is how it can be prevented or delayed.

Chapter VIII

Conserving Social Strength

We have seen that the quality which draws serious adherents to a movement and makes its message meaningful is the demand it imposes on those who want to be part of it. The higher that demand, the more serious and fewer the adherents and the more meaningful the message, at least to them. We have noted that high-demand movements have lifted their members to almost superhuman achievements while stirring up a certain turbulence along the way. And we have observed the ebbing away of demand during the life-course of a movement until it sinks to the level of the environing population. Now we can consider Wesley's question: Is there no way to prevent this decay of pure religion? Or if it cannot be prevented, *is there no way that aging religious organizations can be rejuvenated, regenerated, resurrected?* How did they get started in the first place? If it could be done once, why can't it be done again?

Of course, the great religious movements weren't "done"—in the sense of being instigated or contrived. Rather they emerged, happened, appeared when and where a John Wesley, a George Fox, a Joseph Smith, an Elijah Muhammed, was carried away with an inspiration he could not contain. "The Spirit bloweth where it listeth" is as good a way to sum it up as any. Still, we might consider what it takes to get a religious movement going. Anyone proposing to regenerate or replace declining religious organizations by pumping up new ones should realize the magnitude of his proposition. He is asking someone to take on years of intense struggle and striving during every waking hour, backbreaking responsibility, heartbreaking frustration, scorn, ridicule, and persecution, with perhaps a tragic martyrdom at the end.

It will not be easy to hire someone for *this* job description, even with a salary and expense account worthy of an antipoverty warrior. In fact, there is probably not money enough in the world to pay someone to work up a new religion of the kind that will make a difference. Only those who cannot escape an inner compulsion that burns along their bones like Jeremiah's[1] will subject themselves to the glorious and protracted anguish of gathering a religious movement and leading it through trial and torment to—respectability. Even if one were found willing to work and strain and suffer for the rest of his life to initiate a new religious movement, it is far from certain that he would succed. Such investment is necessary—but may not be sufficient—to achieve the desired end. Some there are who have paid the price but did not gain the prize. How many more are there whose names we do not know?[2]

Renewing Existing Churches

But perhaps it is not necessary to start from scratch. Could not a rejuvenator build on what already exists? That is certainly a possibility hallowed by a thousand noble precedents and offering the best hope for reversing the decline of existing bodies. In very few instances has the level of commitment of an existing religion been raised uniformly by a mild increase in the general demand. Religious leaders are constantly exhorting their followers to measure up more fully to the expectations of their faith, with as little

1. "If I say, 'I will not mention Him or speak any more in His name,' there is in my heart as it were a burning fire shut up in my bones, and I am weary with holding it in, and I cannot" Jer. 20:9 (RSV).

2. Elmer T. Clark, *The Small Sects in America* (New York: Abingdon, 1937) lists innumerable tiny groups of believers led by a charismatic founder which lasted only a few years or counted only a handful of converts and then faded away with barely enough effect to be recorded in a researcher's catalog.

success as Brigham Young experienced in trying to renew Mormon devotion sufficiently to boycott the gentiles. Renewal does not take hold unless it is embodied, exemplified, lived out by a particular group, who show the way to a stronger faith by taking it themselves.

That is the course followed by most of the successful reformers. Thus Benedict of Nursia founded the Benedictine Order on a strict monastic rule at Monte Cassino around 529.

The Benedictine Order was in turn purified by the strict reform centered in the monastery of Cluny under its first and second abbots, Berno and Odo, beginning around 910.

In the next century the Cistercian Order, of even greater strictness, grew under the leadership of Stephen Harding and Bernard of Clairvaux.

The Dominicans, Franciscans, and Jesuits were likewise religious orders or societies led by men of new vision of what the church should be—Dominic, Francis of Assisi, and Ignatius Loyola, respectively—raising the level of commitment in the church as a whole.

These movements typify the *ecclesiolae in ecclesia* (little churches within the church) which have infused new vigor and resilience into the churches throughout the centuries. The Roman Catholic Church has shown exceptional ingenuity in harnessing and internalizing these reform movements for the good of the Church as a whole through the device of the religious order existing alongside the secular (parish and diocesan) structure but largely independent of it. Thus the *ecclesiola*, responsible directly to the Pope rather than to the local bishop, served as a legitimated but not subservient source of example, criticism, goading, and competition to the rest of the Church. It raised the general level of demand and commitment by its own greater strictness (an injection of new stringency rather than an imposition of stricture), but it also felt the equal and opposite reaction of the resistant environing mass.

One form of that reaction was the *domestication* of the *ecclesiola*. For example, the central demand posed by Francis of Assisi and the Franciscan Order at its inception (c. 1210) was absolute voluntary poverty, which attracted thousands of adherents within a few years. Yet not long after his death in 1226 the order was divided between those who insisted upon collective—as well as individual —poverty (later called the Observant or strict branch) and those who held that money, buildings, and land could be acquired on behalf of the order and used by its members (the Conventual or looser branch).[3] For the latter, the actual voluntary deprivation of creature comforts which Francis had preached was relaxed, its demand tamed, its renewing effect vitiated.

Another form the reaction took was the *expulsion* of the *ecclesiola*. This happened with Peter Valdez or Waldo and his followers, who petitioned the Third Lateran Council in 1179 for permission to preach repentance and apostolic poverty (much as Francis would preach thirty years later), but was refused. He went ahead notwithstanding and attracted a growing following, for which he was excommunicated by Pope Lucius III in 1184. Nevertheless, the movement grew in northern Italy and thence spread to other parts of Europe, despite efforts of the Church both to repress and to coopt it. It became the Waldensian movement—a vigorous lay Protestantism more than three centuries before Luther's Reformation (which likewise might have remained within the Church if it had not been expelled).

An evicted *ecclesiola*, however, is no longer *in ecclesia*; for our purposes, it is on its own, having virtually to start from scratch. Even when it remains within the environing church, its revitalizing effect is achieved through new or renewed strictness, and its work is not easy. It requires much of the same intense dedication, arduous toil, and rigorous discipline that starting a new movement does. It meets much of the same resistance and generates similar friction against those whom it would bestir out of their sloth.

Lifting the level of men's commitment to meaning is the hardest work there is, and there is no shortcut or gimmick that will make it any easier, whether inside or outside the existing churches. What costs little, accomplishes little. The greater the effect desired, the greater the effort required to achieve it. And there is no effect

3. Williston Walker, *History of the Christian Church, rev. ed.* (New York: Charles Scribner's Sons, 1954), pp. 257 ff.; this is also the source for the entire discussion of *ecclesiolae*.

greater than the enlistment of men in the service of meaning—what some would call the saving of souls. If it were easy, it would not be salvation.

Can Communes Survive?

One of the most exciting and hopeful of man's social traits is the propensity to start up new societies within society, little colonies of innovation, such as those which today are called communes. A handful of people who are disillusioned with the existing social order or inspired with a vision of the ideal society go off together and set up a new community in which relationships are arranged as they *ought* to be. It may be no more than a dozen individuals inhabiting the same abandoned farmstead, but the act of forsaking accustomed ways and collectively exploring and embodying something new exerts a constant fascination that can become irresistible in periods of discontent. This may be keenly felt in accounts of contemporary communes, of which more than two thousand are said to exist at present.[4]

The propensity of little bands of men and women to set up a new way of life together is equalled only by their inability to keep it going. Innovative communities of the past have come and gone so quickly that it is hard to keep track of them. In the nineteenth century there were about a hundred such collectivist settlements in the United States, of which about fifty left sufficient traces for comparison, offering a model in microcosm of the connection between strictness and social survival. F. A. Bushee, writing in the *Political Science Quarterly* in 1905,[5] makes the following observation: some fourteen Owenite colonies were formed around 1825 to embody the socialistic teaching of Robert Owen; these lasted an average of seventeen months. About 1843 another group of such communities was set up in a dozen states following the

4. Robert Houriet, *Getting Back Together* (New York: Coward, McCann and Geoghegan, 1971).
5. 20:625-61.

ideas of Charles Fourier. These twenty-seven Fourierist "Phalanxes" were somewhat more rigorously structured than the Owenite settlements, and they lasted on the average about thirty-one months. Bushee also identifies about twenty "cooperative societies" around the turn of the century, to which he attributes an average life of a little over four years. The fourth group contains what he calls the oldest and most successful communities: the religious colonies, over twenty in number, which lasted an average of twenty-four years, with the six most important ones surviving for an average of ninety-five years!

The first three groups were secular, and among them Bushee listed only three as lasting more than twenty years: Icaria (40 years), Fairhope (33), and the Woman's Commonwealth (30+). Of these the last turns out to have been fanatically religious (according to William Hinds[6]); Fairhope was fanatically devoted to the single-tax doctrine of Henry George; and Icaria was a colony of French immigrants led by Etienne Cabet, which settled for seven years in Nauvoo, Illinois, after the Mormons left. Beginning with fifteen hundred members, it dwindled and split and squabbled for almost half a century, marked by a persistence of dogmatism that is religious in its fervor. The president of the Icarian community wrote to Hinds in 1877: "You are perfectly right in supposing that we elevate the principle of communism, and especially the principle of fraternity, into the place of a religion."[7]

The point of this comparison is not that only the devout were blessed with success, since several religious settlements expired as quickly as any nonreligious ones. The variable that seems most closely linked to longevity is not religion as such but the quality often associated with it which we are calling strictness—an element also present to some degree in certain of the more disciplined secular colonies. The Fourierist Phalanxes had more rules than the Owenites, and some of the "cooperative societies" were more carefully regulated (and more homogeneous, as in the case of

6. William A. Hinds, *American Communities and Cooperative Colonies* (Chicago: C. H. Kerr & Co., 1908).

7. *Ibid.*, p. 383.

the dozen or more secular Jewish immigrant socialist settlements) than either the Owenite or Fourierist groups.

In reading about the struggles of these settlements or visiting the sites they inhabited (especially the Shaker communities, the Amana villages in Iowa, or the Oneida Community in upstate New York) one cannot help but feel a pang at their loss. There is a considerable literature about these heroic collective innovations of the last century, and their experience may offer some clues to the survival of the communes which dot our contemporary landscape. In fact, it was the comparison of the quality of organization in the nineteenth-century settlements which helped to suggest the hypothesis developed in the preceding chapters. It is not a simple matter for a group of people to live together in an experimental community for very long, especially as such communities tend to attract experimental people—that is, those attracted to innovation, change, and variety rather than perseverance and stability. Without a significant degree of discipline (which must be mostly *self*-discipline), rigorous organization, and high commitment to common objectives, the average innovative colony all too readily succumbs to rivalries over positions of leadership, resentments over assignment to disagreeable but necessary chores—or failure of anyone to do those chores—and all kinds of petty spites and squabbles. One may expect that contemporary communes will have to meet the same kinds of tests if they are to survive. Those that are stricter will last longer.

An example of the stricter type of commune seems to be "The Children of God," a movement that has swelled within a year from 300 to over 2,000 members, located in 39 colonies in seven countries, but concentrated chiefly in remote rural areas in southern California and west Texas. They have stirred up hostility among churches, parents, and neighbors wherever they have gone because of their fanaticism. Most members are in their twenties, offspring of white middle-class families, who have repudiated their parents, their former career plans and ideas.

The Children live a tightly structured communal life . . . Basic indoctrination classes for new converts last from three to five months. . . . The Children do not even own their own clothing; they salvage anything in the laundry room that fits. They are conservation conscious. . . . They say they are appalled by American wastefulness. . . . They operate kindergarten and elementary schools using the Montessori method. Dating is forbidden. Marriage proposals are offered during an instant of courtship "as God leads" and subject to approval of the elders. . . . Cigarettes, booze, and drugs are taboo. Prayers, not aspirin, are applied to headaches. Television and all magazines and books except the Bible are shunned. . . . Natural childbirth is practiced. Babies are usually placed in the full-time custody of nursery attendants. . . . New converts are admonished to submit themselves entirely to the elders. . . . A "security" system also ires many parents who have been unable on visits to talk with their children alone or to get mail through uncensored. . . . [The Children believe that] a Communist anti-Christ will take over America and persecute Christians. The only Bibles left will be those stored in [their] minds [by memorization]. The "systemite" or establishment Christians will cave in. Only a strongly disciplined remnant will survive to witness for Christ.[8]

The Children often make missionary excursions in dilapidated buses to nearby cities to seek converts among the "street people." Initially welcomed by other "Jesus freaks" and some evangelistic churches, they have alienated most of them by their uncompromising insistence that everything else in life must be rejected in favor of total devotion to their version of Christian discipleship. "He who loves father and mother more than me is not worthy of me" is their characteristic quotation from the Gospel (Matt. 10:37). And for this faith many of them have left not only their parents but the addictions and indulgences of the youthful drug culture.

Why Is Strictness Important?

An examination of religious movements and innovative communities suggest that social strength will not be retained without strictness, and that once strictness has ebbed away (taking with it strength), it is difficult if not impossible to recover. If this is

8. Edward Plowman, "Where Have All the Children Gone?" *Christianity Today,* Nov. 5, 1971, pp. 38-40. See also "Ill Winds Buffet Communal Sect" by James T. Wooten in *New York Times,* Nov. 29, 1971, pp. 41 and 49.

the case, it is not because strictness cannot be newly conceptualized or formulated in regulations, but because it is virtually impossible to apply or enforce in an existing organization. People who have become accustomed to leniency do not find it congenial to contemplate strictness, let alone live under it. Yet—if this analysis is correct—*strictness is the only way to conserve social strength*, whether in *ecclesia* or *ecclesiolae*.

The indispensability of strictness seems to some an ungracious and abrasive prescription, if not incomprehensible. Yet it is simply the necessary corollary and projection of seriousness in what one is doing. Søren Kierkegaard calls it ". . . severity, the severity which is inseparable from the seriousness of eternity."[9] If one is dealing with matters of salvation, of eternity, then it makes a vast difference whether one does what is "right" or its opposite. As religious groups age and mellow, they tend to relax their severity, their strictness, their seriousness. Kierkegaard's *Attack upon Christendom* is a vehement denunciation of the state church of Denmark for its lack of seriousness, or rather, its insistence that seriousness is not necessary to Christianity, which is thereby allowed to degenerate into a smug paganism in which things are called Christian without having to be any different from what they were: "What Christianity wanted was earnestness in living, and to do away with vain honors and glories, [but] everything remained as it was, the change being that it assumed the predicate 'christian': the gewgaws of knightly orders, titles, rank, etc. became 'Christian'—and the priest . . . is tickled to death when he himself is decorated with— the Cross. The Cross! Yes, in the Christianity of 'Christendom' the Cross has become something like the child's hobby-horse and trumpet" (pp. 164–5).

In essay after essay, Kierkegaard contrasts the smooth, bland, effortless, comfortable Christianity of Denmark with the poverty, persecution, rejection, and martyrdom of those who seriously follow the way of true Christianity. "Verily there is that which is more contrary to Christianity . . . than all heresies and all schisms com-

9. Søren Kierkegaard, *Attack upon Christendom* (Boston: Beacon Press, 1956), p. 123.

bined, and that is to *play* Christianity. But precisely in the very same sense that the child plays soldier, it is playing Christianity to take away the danger . . . and in place of this to introduce power (to be a danger to others), worldly goods, advantages, luxurious enjoyment. . . ." (pp. 7–8). He uses the word leniency to describe the "common Christianity in the land" (p. 37), and exclaims: "When one sees what it is to be a Christian in Denmark, how could it occur to anyone that this is what Jesus Christ talks about: cross and agony and suffering, crucifying the flesh, suffering for the doctrine, being salt, being sacrificed, etc.? No, in Protestantism, especially in Denmark, Christianity marches to a different melody, to the tune of 'Merrily we roll along, roll along, roll along'—Christianity is enjoyment of life, tranquillized. . . ." (pp. 34–5).

Kierkegaard was calling Christians to be serious about their faith, but the same element may apply to other content: Mormon or Muslim or Marxist. We can now try to generalize what would seem to be the minimal degree of seriousness in any religious or quasi-religious movement.

Minimal Maxims of Seriousness (Strictness)

Those who are serious about their faith:

1. Do not confuse it with other beliefs/loyalties/practices, or mingle them together indiscriminately, or pretend they are alike, of equal merit, or mutually compatible if they are not.

2. Make high demands of those admitted to the organization that bears the faith, and do not include or allow to continue within it those who are not fully committed to it.

3. Do not consent to, encourage, or indulge any violations of its standards of belief or behavior by its professed adherents.

4. Do not keep silent about it, apologize for it, or let it be treated as though it made no difference, or should make no difference, in their behavior or in their relationships with others.

Members of a student Christian organization could see no reason why their Jewish friends should be excluded from membership in the group. Yet some of them who were also members of an organization working for immediate U.S. withdrawal from Vietnam had objected to the inclusion in that group of persons who felt that gradual withdrawal of U.S. forces within two years was the best that could be obtained. The objection to their membership was that they didn't really support the aims of the immediate-withdrawal organization, so why should they be admitted? Obviously, these students were more *serious* about immediate withdrawal from Vietnam than they were about Christianity.

That is not to say that adherents of Judaism or exponents of gradualism are inherently inferior—or superior—to, or in any nonpertinent respects different from, Christians or immediate-withdrawal enthusiasts. But they *are* different in the one respect pertinent to the organization(s) in question: *they do not support its objectives.* To take them into membership anyway is to show a lack of seriousness about the organization; it is to invite the contempt both of those admitted and of nonmembers. It is to reduce the force of the group's objectives (even if the new members do not actively oppose them) and consequently the willingness of any of the members to struggle and sacrifice for them. Yet this is precisely the kind of promiscuity of membership that many American churches have engaged in for a century or more—and people wonder why they are declining!

The same student Christian organization was appalled at the suggestion that one of the members who had been caught stealing from the campus bookstore should be expelled or suspended from the group. "What has that got to do with it?" they demanded. Yet some of them who also belonged to an Ecology Society were in no doubt that members of that group found littering should be drummed out of the corps immediately. Obviously, they were more *serious* about ecology than they were about Christianity—which is their privilege, but it points up which of the two organizations was stronger, and why. Strictness proved their seriousness and created strength among the ecologists; leniency evidenced a lack of seriousness and contributed to organizational weakness among the Christians.

It is not necessary to embrace ecology or Christianity in order to compare the social strength of their organizations. Though he might not have as rich a historical store of total demand and heroic martyrdom to call upon, another Kierkegaard could have written an equally scathing critique of halfhearted Druids. The principles of seriousness we are considering apply to any company or group seeking to achieve an objective, and *a fortiori* to any *religious* body. They merely draw the logical implications of purpose and efficacy.

If a voluntary association is formed to abolish capital punishment, it does not knowingly include among its members those who *favor* capital punishment. They are free to form their own association, which in its turn will exclude advocates of abolition. Both groups will be especially careful to limit the inner circles of leadership to those who wholly support the organization's objectives. For the abolitionists to include a couple of advocates of the death penalty on their executive committee for the luxury of giving the opposition equal time would be to introduce into their efforts a counterforce that would seriously reduce their own effectiveness, like a jet plane trying to fly with one of its engines reversed. Yet just such fatuousness is indulged every day by groups that ought to know better.

Many there are, apparently, who confuse a church with a lodge or social club (and most lodges and social clubs are more particular about whom they admit than some churches are). By admitting new members for the pleasure of their company and the welcome addition of their contributions, the church is reduced to the condition of a lodge or social club which has little to bind its members together except fellowship—and a fellowship all too easily disrupted by disagreement or difficulty. This clubbiness of churches has come about because members deem it churlish to refuse any of their friends admittance, thus confusing friendship with the qualifications for membership that should apply in any seriously purposive group, particularly a religious group. Such standards are considered ungracious when they are not understood and appreciated as necessary effectuations of serious purpose. Strictness has been much misunderstood because in the past it has often been overapplied, with excessive harshness. Perhaps its good name can be somewhat restored if necessary elements can be distinguished from the extreme.

At one time it was thought that religious beliefs or practices which differed from those of the dominant group (then the established church(es), both Protestant and Roman Catholic) must be denounced, anathematized, stamped out, and their adherents sequestered, exiled, or executed. Pope Innocent III in 1209 proclaimed a crusade against the heretical Cathari of southern France that went on for twenty years, during which thousands of men, women, and children were outlawed and slaughtered at will by rapacious freebooters who then confiscated their property. To consolidate the results of this crusade, the Inquisition was instituted by the Synod of Toulouse in 1229 and perfected by Pope Gregory IX, who made it the standard instrument for rooting out heresy. Its most intensive application, however, was in Spain beginning in 1480, when Ferdinand and Isabella used it (despite the protests of Pope Sixtus IV) as a device for suppressing dissent, consolidating their power, and confiscating property for the crown. Even after the Protestant Reformation began, dissent was punished by death. Miguel Servetus wrote a book denouncing the concept of the Trinity, for which he was condemned to be burned by Roman Catholic authorities in Lyons, but he escaped to Calvin's Geneva —where in 1553 he was arrested and burned at the stake by the Protestants.

This kind of thought-control has proved both unsuccessful and unnecessary. It did not keep heterodoxy from spreading, and heterodoxy did not pose so great a threat to the *civil* order as had been supposed. Civil rulers finally concluded that men could be permitted to differ freely about the Trinity—and many other matters— without being subjected to the rack or stake. Thus gradually civil tolerance of dissent grew into genuine freedom of speech, press, and assembly. In modern Western nations, at least in theory and claim, men are not prosecuted or punished by the civil authority for their beliefs, speeches, publications, or associations, but only for overt acts that threaten a "clear and present danger" to public health and safety.

The Power of the Gate

Yet many people misapply this essential and excellent canon of civil liberty to the internal affairs of voluntary organizations, which do not command the force of civil authority. They have only one means by which to preserve their purpose and character, and that is the power of the gate—to control who may enter and remain and on what conditions. And the gate swings only one way: it cannot compel anyone to become or remain a member for one minute against his will. Therefore it is crucial that this very mild and limited power be used with great care and seriousness if the organization is to protect itself against diversion, subversion, and deterioration.

The Anabaptists and Wesleyans can give us guidance in shaping and preserving the integrity of the religious organization without violating the dignity or integrity of persons.

a. They were in no haste to take anyone into membership. A long period of training and preparation preceded admission, during which the rigors and privations of discipleship, especially real in the sixteenth century, were vividly described and the candidate warned away if he was not willing to incur them. Various tests of readiness were passed and solemn vows taken in the presence of the congregation to show that he knew what he was getting into and made his choice with full awareness and determination.

b. The tests of membership were attitudinal and behavioral rather than solely or chiefly doctrinal. Members had to "know the music as well as the words." They had to understand, feel, express, and *live* the spirit of humility, nonviolence, "resistlessness," etc., which marked the movement. Theirs was not just an acceptance of the present content of the faith but an ardent willingness to pursue it in its future unfolding, to search the Word of God together in utter seriousness and to obey its implications in their lives with total dedication. The early Wesleyans are described as "earnestly groaning for redemption," as in Romans 8:23.

c. *Membership was conditional upon continuing faithfulness.* Spiritual discipline was vigorously applied among the Anabaptists: any member found walking contrary was admonished, and if he did not reform was charged in the congregation, which could impose the ban in varying degrees up to exclusion. A like policy is announced at the end of the General Rules of the Wesleyan Societies (which rules are a model of seriousness and strictness): "These are the General Rules of our societies. . . . If there be any among us who observes them not, who habitually breaks any of them, let it be known unto them who watch over that soul as they who must give an account. We will admonish him of the error of his ways. We will bear with him for a season. But, if then he repent not, he hath no more place among us."[10] It is not known when this practice was last observed in the Methodist churches, but it was probably at least a century ago.

d. *Members made their life pilgrimage together in small groups, aiding and encouraging one another.* No one worked out his salvation in isolation; each was surrounded and sustained by the brethren. If a new problem arose for which they did not know the best course to take, they would earnestly search the Scripture together and discuss it in the congregation until they reached a consensus, with every member taking part. Thereafter, the consensus was not just a matter of choice or taste; since it had been formed by all members, it was binding on all.

Such a group is described and prescribed in the beginning of the Wesleyan General Rules:

Such a society is no other than "a company of men having the form and seeking the power of godliness, united in order to pray together, to receive the word of exhortation, and to watch over one another in love, that they may help each other to work out their salvation."

That it may the more easily be discerned whether they are indeed

10. *The Book of Discipline of the United Methodist Church* (1968), para. 95, p. 51.

working out their own salvation, each society is divided into smaller companies, called *classes,* according to their respective places of abode. There are about twelve persons in a class, one of whom is styled the *leader.* It is his duty,

1. To see each person in his class once a week at least, in order: (*a*) to inquire how his soul prospers; (*b*) to advise, reprove, comfort, or exhort, as occasion may require: (*c*) to receive what he is willing to give toward the relief of the preachers, church and poor.

2. To meet the ministers and the stewards of the society once a week, in order: (*a*) to inform the minister of any that are sick, or of any that walk disorderly and will not be reproved; (*b*) to pay the stewards what he has received of his class in the week preceding.

This remarkable structure for mutual aid and reinforcement has not been in effect in Methodist churches for generations, but their members are still occasionally able to experience some of the benefits thereof in "sensitivity-training groups."

e. No one who had not undertaken the rigorous training and accepted the obedience and discipline of the group had any voice in making the decisions of the group. This was not to disparage the worth of outsiders, but to make a distinction necessary to every group that seeks to maintain its identity: between those who belong and those who do not. That distinction has become increasingly blurred in many churches, usually due to carelessness or casualness, but in some recent instances because of a curious ethical quandary. Some churches have felt themselves called to minister to the poor, the sick, prison inmates, and so on, as part of their obedience to the Christian mission portrayed in the parable of the Good Samaritan. As a result, their charitable ministries have grown in size and in the number of persons served. Now come many of those who have been beneficiaries of the churches— and whom the churches have taken pride in not trying to convert to their own views—and demand a voice in "making the decisions that affect their destiny."

For instance, a congregation has invited members of a neighborhood youth gang to use the church gymnasium on weekdays; the gang now demands representation on the governing board of the church, although its members are not members of the church and do not (necessarily) intend to become such. If the church resists such an arrangement, it is accused of "paternalism," "colonialism," and "exploitation," for manipulating other people's lives without giving them a hearing. If the church offers a hearing, it is not enough, since the actual decisions are still not being made by the persons affected. Only full voting membership will suffice. And in response to such demands, church mission boards are actually taking into voting membership the representatives of various minorities—blacks, Indians, Chicanos, students—whose individual claims to prior bona fide membership in the church are not always clear. It is easier to see how the churches got into this dilemma than to see how they can get out, yet one has the feeling that the Anabaptists would have had an answer to such demands. It would have been to welcome the protestors as applicants for membership and start them on the lengthy course of preparation all members must undergo before becoming eligible to vote in the church. In fact, if the church is serious about its business, there can be no other answer. If this becomes the basis for charges of proselytizing, the churches may need to close their charitable or educational institutions or set them free—remove them from church connection and support.

Seriousness about one's faith-commitment need not mean a refusal to recognize the existence of other, differing faith-commitments on the part of other persons, or the validity and bindingness of their commitments, for them. It does not preclude respect for such commitments and regard for those who hold them. On the other hand, such respect and regard does not necessarily mean the withholding of missionary zeal, even though it may—perhaps unjustifiably—be resented. Seriousness about one's commitment need not prevent cooperation with persons of differing commitments in enterprises of mutual concern, but a serious and thoroughgoing faith-commitment of the kind we have been considering seems to occupy, preoccupy, and preempt most of the time, energy, and interest of those caught up in it. There might in theory be no obstacle to a Jehovah's Witness working with non-Witnesses in defense of religious freedom, for instance. The Witnesses were the beneficiaries of a series of important cases brought in their behalf by the American Civil Liberties Union in the 1930's, yet never made anything that could be called common cause with their non-Witness defenders. In fact, Stroup describes what is probably the typical outlook of strong faith-groups upon other organizations: "Once in speaking with Mr. Arthur Gaux, a member of the Board of Directors, I reminded him . . . that the American Civil Liberties Union had voluntarily aided the Society on many occasions in their legal problems. Mr. Gaux promptly told me in a rather curt way that the Society did not 'care a hoot' about the American Civil Liberties Union or any other organization. He said that if the Union cared to assist the Society it could, but that the Society did not recognize any obligation toward it. The Union, said Mr. Gaux, was not led by Jehovah and unfortunately did not have 'the truth.' "[11]

One finds it difficult to envision Jehovah's Witnesses (or similar groups) working individually or collectively with non-Witness persons or groups on anything. They simply are not interested in any objectives other than "witnessing"—which they alone can do.

The Hazards of Chosen-Peoplehood

When one notes that secular organizations are wary of too close identification with other, competitive secular bodies for fear of losing their distinctive appeal, it should not be surprising that an even sharper sense of identity pervades strong faith-groups. It is not intrinsically a matter of hostility, snobbishness, or lack of fellow feeling (although it may sometimes seem so, as in the case of Mr. Gaux cited above), so much as it is of being absorbed, and exhausted in the intensive collective experience of the high-demand faith-organization. The rest of the world, with its needs and causes, has little reality except as relatively passive target, grist or vineyard. It is not looked upon as a source of meaningful initiative or activity.

11. Stroup, *The Jehovah's Witnesses* (New York: Columbia University Press, 1945), p. 126.

However much we may try to make more rational and acceptable —more "liberal"—the exclusiveness of high-demand movements, we cannot disguise the fact that any such group of people *in motion* is not inclined to tarry along the way for idle chitchat with bystanders. They are instead intent on *going somewhere*, reaching the goal, running the race that is set before them, delivering the message entrusted to their care. As long as they are moving along in a body, there will be unavoidable turbulence between them and the stationary populace—or rather a general populace whose members are milling about in what seems by comparison a random, atomistic Brownian motion. The concerted movement cleaves its way through the throng, but it is dependent upon concert, upon cohesion within itself, which in turn depends upon the members' consciousness of being somehow special—different, distinct from "everybody else." That consciousness of specialness, of chosen-peoplehood, is a never-failing irritant to others.

The Jews were disliked and persecuted from early times, in part at least because of their insistence that God had "chosen" them (whether chosen for privilege or for suffering is immaterial to the consequences)—that they were somehow set apart and could not intermarry with, or even *eat* with, the unchosen. Can one imagine anything more likely to stir up hostility and outrage? Or to inspire persecution? Ghetto walls usually have two sides, and in this instance the building began on the inside, during the postexilic period, as a mechanism for preserving the identity of the Chosen People. It succeeded magnificently. Christians are not excused for their vicious persecution of Jews through the centuries by the recognition that in the turbulence surrounding any group in motion, any "chosen people," there is the possibility of the whirlwind.

The early Christian Church experienced the same disturbance. Terming itself *ec-clesia* or "called-out" (from the rest of society), it set itself apart from the unsaved pagan world. One finds in the early letters of Paul and in Acts the record of the struggle to understand and formulate this separateness. It was gradually decided that Christians might, within certain limits, eat and associate with non-Christians in daily life, but their cult life remained completely exclusive. Not only would they not participate in the pervasive religious activities of their neighbors, but they would not admit outsiders to their own sacred rites. Even those undergoing the extensive preparation for membership (catechumens) could attend only the first part of the Mass and were excluded from the later and more sacred portion. This secrecy inspired all manner of suppositions among non-Christians about the scandalous nature of the clandestine ceremonies engaged in, and such rumors fed the flames of persecution.

In all such groups it is their set-apartness that imparts and maintains their social strength, infuriates their neighbors, and earns them ostracism and persecution. In fact, *their social strength is proportionate to the difficulty of getting in and staying in and to the number of manifest distinctions* (stigmata) *between those who belong and those who do not.* This rudimentary correlation between chosen-peoplehood and social strength seems obvious, but it continues to engender hard feelings and resentments. It may help to explain some of our perplexities about the seeming obnoxiousness of some religious groups.[12]

The most Orthodox Jews seek to maintain their exclusive and dominant position in Israel because (in their view) they and only they are the true and faithful embodiment of the Chosen People.

The most "religious" Christians in the Glock-Stark study are also the most anti-Semitic, for the same reason that they are also the most anti-Moslem, anti-Buddhist, and anti-any-other-body-than-their-own; because the differences between their faith-group and others are more important to them than they are to less "religious" Christians.

Southern Baptists and Missouri-Synod Lutherans are less tolerant of dissident theologians than more ecumenical bodies because correctness and uniformity of belief is more important to them: since they are blessed with the Truth, any departure from it within the ranks is less tolerable than it would be to groups whose view of truth is more relative and permissive.

The Pope's reassertion of a hard line on birth control, abortion,

12. See Chapter II.

and celibacy, as well as the Episcopalians' firm position on apostolic succession and the Methodists' continuing insistence on abstinence from alcohol—these are all vestiges of pre–ecumenical strictness: efforts to preserve at least a few of the distinguishing beliefs and practices that make their groups special and give them their unique character and identity.

Perhaps at this point we can summarize some of the salient conclusions from the foregoing:

1. A group is not inclined to cooperate with other groups until it has lost many of the traits of strictness that accompany and conserve social strength.

2. A group that begins to cooperate with other groups will begin to lose any traits of strictness or evidences of social strength it may still have.

3. For all practical purposes, there is no means by which the deterioration of social strength in a given organization can be slowed or arrested except by a reassertion of strictness.

Chapter IX

The Conservative Role
of Religion

Many renewal-minded theologians are welcoming the institutional decline of the churches because of the possibilities for constructive change it opens in an otherwise impenetrable structure. They see visions of new kinds of holy community other than the traditional parish, presbytery, or diocese; new forms of mission, new life-styles of discipleship. They point to the emergence (particularly among young, educated Roman Catholics) of an "underground church," etc.[1]

These are hopeful signs, but it is not the first time they have appeared. Discontents, improvisations, and innovations in religion are not new and will not cease so long as men are religious—which, I have contended in an earlier chapter, will be quite a while. Whether the new religious groupings are equalitarian or hierarchical, sacramentarian or mystical, primitivist or sophisticated, celibate or hologamous, pietistic or crusading, apocalyptic or ecological, may be less significant for their survival than their social strength, their seriousness, their strictness, as described in the foregoing chapters.

Many of man's contemporary maladies are in the realm of meaning and are therefore susceptible to treatment only in that realm. The prevailing patterns for communicating ultimate meanings

1. See, for example, Rosemary Reuther's "The Vanishing Religious Order and the New Human Community," *Christian Century*, April 7, 1971, pp. 425 ff.

(churches) are not functioning at their full potential, and better bearers of such meanings are desperately needed today. We can look to these new developments with hope, anxiety, and a certain degree of skepticism: hope, because they bear the brightest promise of what is needed; anxiety, lest they be unable to manifest and maintain the seriousness worthy of that promise and essential to its survival; and skepticism as to the staying power of persons attracted to protests, reforms, and innovations.

Neglect of Meaning

The new religious groupings (I shall not refer to them as movements until they begin to *move* with the coherence, force, and directionality described in the last chapter) all too often show a lack of confidence in the efficacy of the stock-in-trade of religion, which is meaning. Many a grouplet in the churches which has gathered itself around the banner of civil rights, or the war on poverty, or community organization, or preserving the biosphere, seems to feel that the best contribution churchmen can make to the cause is one indistinguishable from what a secular group might make. That is known in some circles as being relevant to the felt needs of the world; but some of the needs the world feels may not be its real and underlying needs. Religious groups should not abdicate their unique and essential contribution to healing the world's wounds: *meaning.*

Several years ago, the relevant thing for churches to do was to "combat poverty." Under that banner, many churchmen seemed to lose their sense of how the churches combat poverty—if they ever had it. So in an article which appeared in the *Christian Century* I tried to suggest the churches' proper function. Although written in "Christian" language, with specifically Christian assumptions and terminology, it can readily be translated into the more general terms of this book and illustrates how a particular meaning-system might direct itself to a specific problem. It began with a Scriptural illustration developed by a former pastor of mine, Morgan Phillips.

Peter and John were walking in the temple at the hour of prayer. Beggars were pleading for alms as usual, and one who daily lay at the gate asked their help. What is the *Christian* answer? . . . the conventional morality tale would propose one or another of several exemplary endings:

(1) They could give the beggar some money;

(2) They could help him find some useful employment suitable for the handicapped;

(3) They could encourage him through various supportive techniques to overcome his personal problems and recover his self-respect;

(4) They could even explore the possibilities of obtaining . . . therapy which would eliminate his disability.

Possibly any one or all of these responses might have proved helpful, but the two disciples made none of them. Instead, Peter replied, *"I have no silver and gold, but I give you what I have; in the name of Jesus Christ of Nazareth, walk!"*[2]

Which, being translated into the more generalized terms of our argument, insists that religious organizations have a contribution to make to the human predicament that is different from the technological interventions of secular groups. The distinctively religious contribution is to give *meaning* to the situation: purpose, promise, and possibility. That does not mean that meaning should displace technological remedies—men still need food, shelter, clothing, jobs, education, medical care—or even view them as inferior to meaning. And if society or its secular agencies cannot provide the needed technological remedies, religious organizations may need to do so, but with the recognition that such stopgap measures are a distraction and diversion from their distinctive and indispensable service: making sense of the life of man.

But this service does not seem to be enough for some religious leaders—"they want to dash in 'where the action is' and help do whatever needs doing: 'Here, fellows, let me hand out those blankets!' They sometimes seem a little impatient and embarrassed to be standing around with nothing to offer but words when everyone else is busy dispensing layettes, birth-control pills or surplus foodstuffs. . . . They want to 'get into the act too' in some more

2. "The Church and the Anti-Poverty Program," *Christian Century,* June 8, 1966, p. 741.

immediately productive way. Yet they may thereby be neglecting or withholding the very ingredient without which the rest will not hold together!"[3]

Oscar Lewis, in his classic study of a "poverty culture," *The Children of Sanchez,* shows that the poor often have a chance to work, even have a few coins to jingle in their pockets. What they do with these opportunities determines whether they remain poor, and that depends upon what they believe life is all about, what man is supposed to do and be. If he lives only for the present and only for himself, then the money he gets will go to buy a few hours' surcease from misery rather than a bed for his family. On the other hand, if man has a high and continuing worth, he will be able to endure and surmount hunger and handicap, squalor and privation, and has repeatedly done so.

Contrary to the impression given by many contemporary churches, the true business of the genuinely *religious* organization is not baby-sitting or entertainment, not social work or social action, not even what passes for religious education or theology, unless these activities are the means for acting out or otherwise communicating the *meaning* of life which the religious group wants to proclaim.

This is not necessarily a reactionary role for religion; it can be very radical. But it should not be misunderstood. It does *not* mean that the church's business is saving souls rather than social action. Either of these can be the means to, or effect of, proclaiming the meaning of life; both can be a substitute for, or diversion from, that proclamation. Neither does it mean that the religious group's business is "spiritual" or "sacred," and that it should leave material, temporal, secular affairs to those who—allegedly—understand them better. This is a common confusion between treatment and subject matter.

The subject matter of religion is *the entire life of man and whatever affects him.* But the distinctively religious treatment of that subject matter is not technological so much as *meaning-oriented —how can the life of man be understood, its meaning perceived, developed, celebrated, and enhanced?* This treatment may well

3. *Ibid.*

have its technological implications and consequences—it may even be couched, if nothing better offers, in the not-very-evocative terms of technology—but it is not finally aimed at technological considerations. One religious group may preach the necessity of contraception and another opposition to it; both are talking about a technological mechanism for controlling population, but each is doing so as an implication and illustration of what it believes about the meaning of human life and how that meaning is best honored and enhanced. If its message is understood only in the technological dimension, then the religious group has grievously failed in its *religious* mission, which is in the dimension of meaning.

That is precisely where many churches fail today. One young lady of my acquaintance, who was an organizer for Saul Alinsky for a while and has since completed law school in order to struggle in the courts for social change, has little use for the churches, not because they are not radical enough, but because they are not religious enough! "When my friends want to talk about the meaning of life," she complains, "about whether to bring children into the world, we have to gather in one of our homes for a kaffee-klatch rather than at the church; the church isn't really struggling with those questions in any way that would help us."

Not all the blame should be placed on the churches, however. Some boys at a summer church camp had been engrossed in a long and serious bull-session with their college-age counselor about the Meaning of Life. As they parted to go to their cabins one of them asked rather bitterly, "Why don't they ever talk about these things in our church back home?" and the others echoed, "Yeah, why don't they?"

The counselor replied, "Maybe because you don't *let* them."[4]

It is not a question of blame but of failure of function. Churches used to have ways of talking about the ultimate meaning of life— even to twelve-year-old boys (though not usually very successfully in their case).

But today many churches seem to avoid serious discussions of the meaning of life, perhaps because many of the members would

4. From an incident in the author's "The Un-Service Station," *Christian Century,* June 30, 1971, p. 799.

rather not get involved in any examination of the answers they have precariously accepted or avoided, and don't know quite *how* to talk about what really matters to them. The churches cannot fulfill their proper function until they find and effectuate ways for their members to talk about the meaning of life, to explore it in a climate of mutual confidence and support, to try out together how to celebrate, embody, and proclaim the "explanations" they believe make life worth living. Such ways of struggling with the conundrum of human existence are being worked out in some of the new religious groupings—even as they are preserved in some of the old—where the religious group refuses to be diverted from its distinctive mission in the realm of meaning.

How Groups Are Diverted

There are many ways in which even the most congenial and devoted groups can be diverted from what they set out to be and do. This certainly does not mean that a new and experimental religious enterprise should or can have a blueprint of its mission in advance which will answer all doubts and dilemmas before it has met and struggled with them; quite the contrary. Only by striving with life's unfolding problems do such groups discover who they are and what their mission really is. A sense of purpose is not a detailed plan: it requires constant checking, self-examination, reorientation: "Is this what we set out to do? Will it lead us toward where we want to be or in the opposite direction? How can we handle this problem without becoming something we don't want to be?" Some of the new urban ministries and training centers show great self-awareness and purposiveness in shaping their activities and outlook to embody their chosen mission and not something else.

One way in which religious groups are enticed away from their chosen mission or function is by a device called the united front. It was consciously utilized by the Communist Party during the 1930's to gain control of other organizations or to neutralize them. According to Philip Selznick's scholarly and objective study of these tactics, *The Organizational Weapon,*[5] the first objective

5. New York: The Free Press, 1960.

of the "combat party" was to capture existing organizations and use them for its own purposes. Failing this, its secondary objective was to neutralize or demolish them so that they could no longer compete with it for political leverage. The united-front tactic consists of *the demand that all organizations join together in some broad, commendable crusade that is not very close to the central purpose or function of any of them,* but in which they can consume much of their energy and manpower without getting their own work done. This is not to say that organizations should never cooperate in a common cause, but each must ask itself each time whether it is doing its own work or someone else's.

Religious groups generally have a strong humanitarian concern for the well-being of all men, combined with a vigorous urge to shape and strengthen the moral norms of society. Consequently they are often enlisted in united fronts working for (or against) open housing, gun control, repeal of laws against abortion, reduction of military expenditures, outlawing of pornography, elimination of the death penalty, withdrawal of investments in South Africa, home rule for the District of Columbia, and so on. For the purpose of this argument, it is immaterial whether the front is for one side of an issue or the opposite—the question remains the same: *is this our job?* The answer is sometimes Yes, sometimes No. In every instance the religious group should ask itself in the most hardheaded way, "How will this activity help make clearer the ultimate meaning of life to our members?" If the answer is not fairly obvious, the group should reserve its energies for activities which speak more plainly to its purpose, for otherwise it is allowing that purpose to be subverted and itself to be proportionately weakened. Such subversion is equally a problem to new groups and old, and only a single-minded purposiveness will preserve the strength and character of the organization from dissipation by coalitional promiscuity.

In another place and at another time one might argue the need for broader ecumenical coalitions on behalf of each of the specific goals listed above, and many more. Such a course has abundant advocates already. But one should try to confront the danger of the moment, and the danger that needs to be warned against at *this* moment is not the shallowness of ecumenical commitments to supposedly common social causes but the danger of the *failure of the religious function and the consequent collapse of the religious constituency.*

This warning must be carefully spelled out lest it be misunderstood as a denunciation of the social action undertaken at some cost by the mainline churches. If they have erred, it has not been by undertaking social—even political—action, but by doing so in ways that did not adequately communicate the implications for ultimate meaning to their members. As a social-action specialist, the author has devoted many years to intensive efforts on behalf of some of the causes referred to, but such occupational involvement is irrelevant to the question of whether and how and when such actions conduce to the strengthening or the weakening of the church bodies undertaking them. Conceivably, the churches might feel obliged to undertake them for the good of man even if they knew in advance that it would be to their own disadvantage as institutions. But it is not necessary to concede that social action by churches is intrinsically disadvantageous.

The hazard of involvement arises, of course, from the fact that taking sides on social, political, and economic issues in the real world is apt to threaten the actual or felt interests of those on the other side, some of whom may be church members. They will not take kindly to their church's stepping on their toes. Only a very strong counterinfluence can overcome this understandable resentment: the members' commitment to a shared understanding of what life is all about and what, therefore, is right or wrong in human conduct. In the high-demand religious movements, the commitment is strong enough to overcome all lesser, "worldly" interests. Rather than cursing the abolitionists, the believer will sell or free his slaves if his faith-group tells him it is the right thing to do.

In the major churches today, there is insufficient commitment or discipline to produce such a result. Instead, the members feel severally able to judge the rightness of their church's statements and actions on the basis of whether they feel their own personal secular interests threatened! Or, to give them the benefit of the doubt, they feel able to size up the rightness of its actions by their own individual standards of right and wrong, which may be derived from many sources, some of them incompatible with the church's understanding.

This is not to say that the churches are, or ought to be, the only source of moral norms, or that the members have no right to their own views. But in a strong religious organization—one that is effectively helping its members to understand the ultimate meaning of life—such defensive demurrers do not arise. The members have chosen to be part of a highly demanding, communal stream of shared experience which shapes their understanding of all life—including what is right and what is wrong in society—and they in turn have helped to shape the collective experience and understanding, and their participation reinforces their commitment to it. They do not feel any divergence between the group's understanding of right and their own; if they do, they hasten to correct their own (mis)understanding. They reorient themselves, not in any spirit of subservience or resentment, but rather with willing acceptance of the guidance of the group, however formed, in their interpretation of life's meaning. If they find themselves out of step, they do not blame the group.

Churches and Social Action

As noted earlier, the mainline churches are not in a position to expect this quality of discipline among their members, and have not been for some time. The question then arises how they shall respond to the moral dilemmas posed by society. Shall they say that society poses *no* moral dilemmas on which they should speak and act? Few Western and virtually no authentically Christian bodies would take such a position. Even very conservative groups which denounce the social and political actions of the ecumenically minded bodies have themselves been highly vocal and politically active in opposition to gambling or pornography or "the liquor traffic" or "atheistic communism."[6] So it is mainly a matter of *which* moral issues a group feels require social action.

Shall they say that it is appropriate for churches to enunciate broad moral principles, but the laity should be left to apply them according to their individual inclination in their role as citizens? As Dr. Colin Williams once observed, such a policy would leave the churches and their members free to take any moral position they might choose—*as long as it was ineffectual.* If an action is right, why is it any less right for the church to act corporately in support of it? Why condemn such support to ineffectuality by insisting that it is not to be initiated, organized, coordinated, or focused by the churches? This is to leave all the good tunes to the devil; that is, to relinquish the effective methods of collective, organized social and political action to all groups *but* the churches. Their members may indeed act individually, but they are more likely to be called into action by their labor union, veterans' organization, industrial or trade association, or political party, and therefore to act in accordance with the objectives of those organizations rather than those of the churches. While the churches may agree with the aims of one or another of these secular bodies from time to time, and even commend them to the individual support of their members, there is only one group whose purposes—under this rubric—the churches could never commend for consistent concerted support by their members: their own!

No organization should be expected to condemn itself to such ineffectuality without good reason.

The Incompatibility of Meaning and Force

The arguments usually cited for churchly self-restraint can be divided into two classes: *formal* and *utilitarian.* The first class implies that it is not proper for the church to use the methods of

6. The Rev. Carl McIntyre has made a career of denouncing the political machinations of the national and world councils of churches, yet it was no less "political" for him to lead mass marches on Washington to press the Nixon administration for "Victory in Vietnam."

the world, such as the sword of power, violence, and coercion, because those methods are contrary to some norm such as natural law or God's command. The second class would reach similar conclusions on different grounds: the church should not use certain methods because they will produce results contrary to those desired by the church, or they will be counterproductive or self-defeating. If one receives knowledge from nonexperiential sources such as revelation, one may find the first class of reasons adequate. If one has no such knowledge, then one may seek wisdom or validation in experience. If something is said to be wrong or improper, it should be possible to point to results in human experience which show it to be wrong or improper—counterproductive or self-defeating of desired ends or conditions, or productive of undesired ends or conditions. If there are no evident negative results, then on what basis can it be said to be wrong or improper? Both classes, fortunately, tend to agree on a basic principle which might be generalized in our terms to say: *organizations concerned with meaning do not fulfill their function by using force or coercion.*

This is a sound generalization from human history, and another book could be written illustrating it. Suffice it here to note the basic observed incompatibility between meaning enterprises and power enterprises. This is not to say that power has never been used to impose a given formulation of meaning; many a people has been "converted" to Christianity or Islam by conquest; many have doubtless accepted docilely the truth revealed by the sword. But the economics of meaning is not mocked: the conversion, the acceptance, the truth, were only as deep as the exigencies of the moment required. Frequently the new faith became simply a gloss on the old, which lay unchanged beneath. More often, rebellion and contempt lurked beneath the surface, mocking the conqueror, waiting only for him to turn his back.

Certainly it is true today that any religious organization seeking to gain or keep converts by force is not only pushing a rope of sand uphill but is laying up future trouble for itself. There are situations in which coercion is justifiable, though not necessarily effective, in inculcating meaning. Parents have a right and duty to exercise control over their children, even in matters of meaning.

They may properly require their children to go to church or to read the Bible. Even within this more or less justifiable framework, however, we see that compulsion is often counterproductive, sometimes building up negative feelings against the thing compelled.

It is not force or coercion for a religious body to set standards of membership and to hold members to them. Nor is it force or coercion for religious bodies to preach and proclaim to the best of their ability what social or political actions their members should take, individually *and* collectively. It is even legitimate for the religious body to make adherence to a given standard mandatory, as in refraining from divorce or abortion or birth control or beverage alcohol, and to expel members who do not comply. No one has a *right* to belong to a religious body, particularly if he fails to comply with requirements of membership as that body defines them. Whether members can properly be compelled to vote in civil elections as a church directs is a borderline case, but so long as secret ballots are in use, not one apt to create serious problems of excommunication.

When, however, a religious body threatens a nonmember, such as a civil official, with reprisal—at the polls, for instance, if he does not endorse and enforce their standard of right—then that body is using force and coercion wrongfully and will sooner or later reap the results. The Anti-Saloon League often used this tactic in establishing Prohibition, and perhaps that was one reason the movement failed. To use bribery or blackmail or any other method that is palpably illegal, whoever uses it, is improper—that is, counter-productive and self-defeating—for a religious body, indeed *especially* for a religious body. But it is not improper for such a body to use the same methods of publicity, persuasion, or even pressure that other voluntary groups do: that is, petitions, mass meetings, picketings, even a strike, boycott, ostracism—methods which do not directly damage a person or his reputation or property except by persuading other persons that he is in the wrong. It may not be popular, but it is not contrary to the generalization about what is incompatible with meaning; in fact, it may be necessary to a thoroughgoing embodiment of meaning.

The Role of Reconciliation

Sometimes it is asserted that the use of collective social action by a religious body in behalf of a controversial cause is improper because it makes difficult or impossible that body's acting as a mediator between parties in conflict. Some religious organizations define their own role as one of reconciliation,[7] and so avoid taking actions which would alienate any group. Other bodies feel a prior concern for justice, and so may champion one side or the other in a conflict. Both the reconciler and the advocate make a significant contribution to society, but it is not the same contribution, and the two may be incompatible in the same body. The point is that *each embodies a particular understanding of man and society, a specific explanation of how life is and ought to be.* A religious body should determine which stance is compatible in a given case with its system of meaning, and then *pursue it wholeheartedly*, neither pulling its punches nor blurring its image.

Calling the Faithful into Action

The churches in their present plight cannot look to their members for disciplined adherence to any particular role or meaning, so they are drawn to another option: to proclaim the meaning which the faithful *ought* to see in the social situation, to define the situation in such a way that the membership will recognize their duty and do it, to lift up a lofty standard in the hope that members will rally around it. That is the option which many church leaders have chosen today, but it has not worked out quite as intended. Instead of rallying the faithful round the flag, these leaders have found themselves at a greater and greater distance from their

---

7. So the Archbishop of Canterbury, Michael Ramsey, in criticizing grants by the World Council of Churches to combat white racism: such grants allegedly impair the churches' reconciling role.

ostensible followers, waving the flag more frantically as the gap has widened. Thus the leadership has far outrun the followership, and not necessarily to the discredit of either, but to the loss of both. The situation is a by-product of the general attenuation of meaning in the major churches: the leaders—despite some valiant efforts—have not succeeded in making clear how the social action they invoke fits in with—in fact, is required by—the meaning-system of the church.

So this option may need to be abandoned for another: to *create a community of shared experience and meaning within the churches.* To continue pressing public issues that do not elicit support from the membership can lead only to further alienation of the puzzled faithful, and further discrediting of the committed leadership that is not being followed. It may be that there is no shared meaning in the churches any more. If not, they ought to know it and quit pretending there is such a thing. On the other hand, it may be that there *is* some shared meaning, but that most of the present members are not prepared to endure difficulty or discipline for it, or perhaps they give priority to other meanings they share with the Chamber of Commerce or the American Legion. If so, the churches ought to know it and act accordingly, either to reduce the ranks to those who are willing to meet the standards, or to throw in the sponge and settle for being promiscuous social clubs.

There are some today who urge the churches to build up a new community of shared meaning and let the old community lapse. That is what happened in the *ecclesiolae* of the past and what is being attempted in some new religious groupings at present. But this proposal may underrate the old community and overrate the new, largely because it overlooks the possibility that *there is something intrinsically conservative about the religious enterprise, and this is not necessarily bad.*

Churches as Agents of Change

It is a commonplace today for some of the most concerned and committed young leaders in the churches to address their constituents as "agents of change," calling them to storm the bastions of the status quo and to bring in the new kingdom of righteousness and peace. It has been disillusioning for them to find the rank-and-file membership, by and large, rather recalcitrant to that summons. The members have shown themselves to be more concerned with stability and security than with change, and this is accounted to them as selfishness, timorousness, obduracy, and sloth. Furthermore, they look to their religious organizations to undergird and enhance that stability and security rather than to foment unpredictable innovations, and this is accounted to them as demonic regressiveness. It may be that religious bodies simply do not attract and retain persons interested in change, and the call for change should be directed elsewhere.

The organizations of religion are repositories of the meanings and values that are most ultimate and intimate for their members. They are responsible for treasuring and enhancing, embodying and transmitting the ideals and qualities that earlier generations have found good. As such, they tend to be concerned more with conserving the tried and true than with exploring or experimenting with the new. Perhaps that is not the way some would wish religious groups to be, especially if their occupational lines are cast in the churches or synagogues and they are personally interested in bringing about alterations in society. They will find themselves surrounded by singularly refractory material for their purpose, and may curse the material for being what it is rather than what they think it should be.

The conserving tendency of religious organizations, however, is basically a healthy and valuable trait, which gives coherence and continuity to human society. If there is fault to be found with it, it lies in the fact that religious bodies often uncritically conserve whole patterns of the immediate past rather than preserving selectively the few great goods distilled from many generations. Thus many a prophet is merely trying to call or recall his hearers to the ancient teachings of the faith, but is persecuted for neglecting or rejecting the more familiar and lesser attachments of a generation ago. Many of his hearers regrettably identify the experiences of their childhood as the eternal good which the religious group is expected to conserve rather than more profound and enduring goods from the more distant past. So the religious organization may err, not in being too conservative, but in being not conservative enough!

As I have noted earlier, religious movements have been engines of the most profound and pervasive social changes in human history. But they are not designed to achieve projected social changes. They have been monumental upheavals of the human spirit directed toward religious objectives, of which social change was the more or less incidental by-product. They could no more have been conceived and generated to accomplish specified social reforms than a volcano can be aimed to erupt in such a way as to destroy a slum and thereby advance urban renewal.

To the average contemporary adherent of the mainstream churches—regrettably untutored in the enduring meanings of his professed faith—it is inconceivable that his church should stand for something other than what he himself (often for nonreligious reasons) stands for. He and his fellows have lavished hours and dollars and devotion upon their churches as repositories of what they have found good and wish to hand on to their children. How then can these institutions now propose to go a-whoring after strange, (to them) new gods? It is not the *least* faithful among members who are most concerned to conserve the ancient (i.e., familiar) good, but the *most* faithful—the very pillars of the congregation. And this is precisely what we should expect; if they were not interested in preserving and protecting the good and true and beautiful things of life for posterity, they probably would not be in the church to begin with, let alone at its very center. They would be more likely to devote themselves to business, academia, the arts, or other enterprises in which novelty and change are more welcome. This does not mean that all who are interested in preserving the good, the true, and the beautiful are in the churches, or that all who are in the churches are so concerned. There are conservatives outside the churches, and many persons within them are there for other reasons.

A church or synagogue devoted to social change, then, would be almost a contradiction in terms. This is said in rueful appreciation by one who has pastored several congregations and tried to kindle the flame of reform and regeneration in each, only to have it flicker and fail, more often than not for lack of fuel. These congregations were basically the most devoted and dependable groups imaginable, made up of men and women who genuinely wanted to know what was right and do it (though they did not necessarily accept their pastor's definitions). Some of the laymen I have most trusted and respected have been willing to do almost anything for their beloved church—except rush into the turmoil of social change! Several of them—bless their earnest hearts—remonstrated with me patiently and respectfully for my perverse insistence that Sabbath-observers should be permitted to open their places of business on Sunday if they remained closed on Saturday. "Why, it isn't natural! It would contribute to the commercialization of the Lord's Day!" These were the best men in the congregation: men who *cared* what happened to Sunday. It would have been easier for them to shrug their shoulders and say, "What does it matter? Let them open on Sunday, and we'll have some place to buy the things we forgot to buy during the week." But they wanted instead to preserve the sacred ways as they had found them, even at their own inconvenience. And they could not understand how their pastor could be abandoning the bulwarks of the Holy Faith for the sake of some thin abstractions about justice and religious liberty. They did not try to silence me or make me conform to their expectations; they just wanted to reason with me and let me know how they felt, after which we agreed to disagree—with mutual respect—on Sunday-closing laws, as on some other matters.

In times when social change is the prevailing cry, it is easy to forget the importance of stability, continuity, and predictability. Perhaps social rigidity is the danger of the moment, and an appreciation of the preservation, conservation, and transmission of tried and tested meanings is "out of phase" today. If so, then religious organizations are likewise out of phase, and that may be partly why they are declining. But great institutional orders do not switch their functions with the styles or phases of the day; if they are doing something mankind needs done, they continue to do it. If they falter, it is less likely that they are doing the *wrong* thing than that they are doing the *right* thing *poorly*—at least such is my thesis. And the right thing (in functional terms) for religious organizations to do is to explain life in ultimate terms to their members so that it makes sense. That function is not necessarily or mechanically conservative, but in operation it usually has that effect.

There is no reason why new explanations may not arise that will inspire social change; they have in the past and will in the future. But, as suggested above, the social-change effect is derivative from more central religious concerns, perhaps because social change is essentially a technological enterprise and therefore aimed at problems which are (at least in theory) humanly manageable. It is tangential to the problems with which religion is primarily concerned: those that are both unsatisfactory and unmanageable—i.e., nontechnological problems. To expect religious bodies to occupy themselves with basically technological problems is to divert them from their central work.

More important, however, is the conservative force of the social validation of religious meanings or explanations. As we saw in Chapter IV, it is not just the *content* of these interpretations that makes them persuasive in justifying the ways of God to man, but the stream of shared social experience out of which they arise and in which they are anchored. Their meaningfulness, it was suggested, is determined less by their ideational reasonableness than by the demand they make upon men and the commitment men have given to them, and this investment accumulates over time. When one has invested much of one's labor and devotion in the propagation, protection, and preservation of a given system of meaning and the organization that bears it, one does not lightly give it up for another or even entertain with enthusiasm any suggestions for its modification. Thus the more effective such explanations are—i.e., the greater their validation by investment of human devotion in them over time—the less they will be susceptible or hospitable to change.

This is fundamentally a valuable mechanism; its perversion occurs when the conserving tendency of religious organizations is linked, not to the genuinely enduring meanings that have sustained men through centuries, but to the immediately preceding generation and nostalgia for its good old days, including trivial social customs and conditions that have no necessary connection—or may even have an adverse one—with meaning.

The religious structure at its best praises and perpetuates the reliable continuities of life; it has helped its members through difficult hours of trouble and tragedy; it has bound them together in strength and mutual reinforcement when beset by chaos and catastrophe, peril and persecution; it has upheld them in the face of disease, disaster, and death, and they look upon it as a trusted bulwark against the storms of life. That is its basic business: to be a sustaining and enabling community for its members in confronting the elements in life that are both unpleasant and unavoidable. As such, it attracts and serves and keeps as members those persons who particularly need and value this supportive milieu and who feel and live out a continuing appreciation of and devotion to it.

If now the leaders of that organization expect to summon those members into the struggle for social improvement, they are simply calling the wrong collection of people. The churches and synagogues are not social-action barracks where the troops of militant reform are kept in readiness to charge forth at the alarums and excursions of social change. Rather, they are the conservatories where the hurts of life are healed, where new spiritual strength is nourished, and where the virtues and verities of human experience are celebrated. To rally those within to launch an attack on the status quo is like trying to lead into hand-to-hand combat a collection of nurses, teachers, physicians, and gardeners, people who are capable, responsible, and responsive—at something else.

The Changeableness
of Change-Oriented People

Those who spring into ardent action at the mere mention of a petition or a picket line are not, by and large, in religious organizations, and if they are, the bodies in question are likely to be not very effectively *religious*. Their interests lead them in a different direction—not a better or a worse one, but different. They have their important contribution to make to human society too, but their interests and affinities are not those typically attracted to religious organizations.

To the degree that new religious groupings seek to attract social activists, militant advocates of social change, aficionados of novelty, variety, and innovation, they are doing one or both of two possibly dysfunctional things: they are calling adventurers, fighters, pioneers, wayfarers to serve in the patient, protracted nurturing and preserving function of the conservatory; or they are making of the conservatory something that it was not before. Both may develop interesting combinations, but they also may be inherently unstable.

This is not to say that persons interested in social change have no proper place in churches, far from it. It is saying that if they understand what religious organizations normally—and normatively —*do,* they will be there not specifically for the sake of social transition, but for the sake of what religious societies as such have to offer, which is help in confronting the unavoidable and unsatisfactory elements of human experience, which befall even advocates of social change. This help is offered in the shared system of meaning which is articulated, witnessed to, lived out, promulgated, in the religious community—a *by-product* of which process *may* be: social change!

There may also be a role for religious groupings or *ecclesiolae* devoted to specified social changes, provided someone is willing to expend the effort and anguish needed to launch such an enterprise. It is hard to conceive of a genuine religious movement taking form around open housing, or community organization, or ending the war, or zero population growth, but who is to say it is impossible? Stranger things have happened, though they have usually been strange in the opposite direction: esoteric or apocalyptic rather than mundane or technological. One may, perhaps, be forgiven the conclusions from the foregoing materials: (1) that such a religious movement is unlikely to develop; (2) that religious groupings devoted to social change are unlikely to attain the social strength, seriousness, or strictness that make for organizational survival or the kind of historical impact attributed to religious movements; and (3) that persons attracted to social-change enterprises will tend not to be receptive to the kinds of commitment necessary to maintain any long-term organizational structure: it is simply not their "thing," and perhaps it's just as well.

This last somewhat jaundiced conclusion is derived from repeated, though admittedly limited, personal experience. In trying, both as a pastor and as a church executive, to develop programs that would appeal to those outside the churches (particularly the young, the disillusioned, the impatient), I discovered a sad paradox. Such programs, because of their novelty or unconventionality or controversiality, often offended or alienated those already in the churches, even though they often succeeded in attracting new people from outside. The irony was that the church could rely on the continuing devotion and support of its older members—even though offended—more than it could on the interest of the newcomers for whom it had offended them! When the time came to pay the bills, or to defend the new programs in the congregation, the "swingers" for whose sake they were developed were usually nowhere to be found, while the old-timers were invariably present and sometimes even consented to foot the bills. Others may have had more favorable experience in such circumstances; if so, let us hope theirs is the norm.

The point of this chapter is to suggest what is entailed in undertaking a religious enterprise as distinguished from a project for social improvement, and to indicate certain possible instabilities in attempting to build the former on the somewhat dissimilar interests of the potential supporters of the latter. Those who confuse the two run the risk of losing the comparatively reliable allegiance of the adherents of religious bodies without obtaining loyalty of comparable reliability from a new constituency to take its place— and this is the precise predicament in which many churches find themselves today.

Chapter X

Religion Is Not Always Tame

If the preceding characterization of archetypal religious enterprises is accurate, it poses some perplexing dilemmas for modern man. Man has a deep craving to make coherent sense of his life within a framework of ultimate meaning, and if that craving is not satisfied to a substantial degree for most men, their whole society is in trouble. We have seen that the mechanism by which such ultimate meanings are developed, embodied, propagated, and maintained is the religious movement or organization. And the mechanism is vigorous and effective in direct proportion to certain qualities (absolutism, conformity, fanaticism, strictness, exclusiveness, and so on) which are not very congenial to the cosmopolitan, urban-industrial, highly educated pluralistic society in which it operates today.

The Craving for Meaning Can Be Fierce

At our civilized best, we rightly pride ourselves on being tolerant, open-minded, equalitarian, and respectful of individual differences, rights, convictions, and sensitivities. But there may be a basic and irreconcilable conflict between these valued qualities of civic life and the imperious dynamics that create and sustain meaning. It would not be the first conflict between our modern public decorum and the primitive drives that seek satisfaction through behaviors learned long before the dawn of civilization. Hunger, sex, and aggression are rude forces that often break out of the channels and institutions that are supposed, in this latter day, to make them less disruptive of society and less obnoxious to the neighbors. The craving for ultimate meaning (or the dread of anomie, to look at its obverse side) is likewise very deep and ancient in human experience, and so we should not be surprised if it, too, has its crude, fierce,[1] and elemental aspects, which cannot be totally tamed without rendering the bearer—group as well as individual—effete, emasculated, ineffective.

A human need whose fulfillment has sometimes entailed mutilations, human sacrifices, crusades, and inquisitions should not be classed with parlor games, literary teas, or other amiable indoor recreations. The deplorable enormities occasionally practiced in the name of religion, as well as its regular perversion by rulers to uphold their thrones, testify not only to its rootage in man's primordial past but to the leverage in men's lives that can be exploited today by its unscrupulous manipulators.

Religion vies with sex as a salient manifestation of emotional pathology. The fact that most people's craving for meaning, like their craving for sex, is readily satisfied by a small amount of the mildest, most attenuated and conventional indulgence does not mean that it is a negligible factor in their lives. On the contrary, persistent deprivation or denial of even the average person's modest need is begging for trouble far out of proportion to the cause. Many people today may not be aware of a dearth of religion or meaning in their lives; they may think they have all the ties to the cosmos the modern age affords or needs. Yet the age is also afflicted with proliferating plagues of suicides, addictions, escapes, disorientations, and derangements which may well be the social hysteria (unconscious displacement of symptoms) from a pervasive but unrecognized deprivation of meaning. And one reason for that deprivation may be a reluctance to accept the rigorous qualities that seem to go with a serious quest for meaning.

All this is to emphasize that the meaning function, anthropologically speaking, is crucial business, which most of us are not man-

1. In its classic sense of wild, untamed.

aging very well. In those undertakings where it is being effectively performed, we see elements somewhat out of harmony with our sophisticated, urbane, and meaning-shy civilization. One purpose of this book is to suggest that these qualities of seriousness/strictness are an apparently necessary feature of any effective meaning-venture, and without them it begins to deteriorate.

This suggestion will probably be unacceptable to those who would contend that "Consciousness III" or some other new condition or disposition has freed man from antique ways of conceiving and transmitting meaning. Strictness is merely a hangover from the puritan rigidity of "Consciousness I," they might say. Let us hope so. But a span of ten to twenty years—even such radically changing years as those we are experiencing—is too short a time to accomplish a really significant alteration in basic human needs, processes, and postures. It is too short even to tell whether such a change is *beginning* to take place.[2] It is about the length of time needed to chronicle a change of surface style—a fad.

If the fundamental and long-standing human mode of apprehending and internalizing and projecting ultimate meaning is changing, it is a transformation that will take many generations: not as long as a biological or genetically based transition, of course, but much longer than a shift of styles. There are culturally conditioned elements in religious behavior, and these can and do alter as readily as other basic cultural institutions, on a scale of decades perhaps. But there are also factors in religious behavior— what I have identified as the way human beings generate, consume, and concretize ultimate meaning—that may be more than culturally conditioned. They may be rooted in the way mankind perceives, remembers, and articulates those abstractions from experience which are invested with deep feeling and linked to personal identity.

2. "Imagine insects with a life span of two weeks, and then imagine that they are trying to build up a science about the nature of time and history. Clearly, they haven't seen enough of the seasons to build a model on the basis of a few days of summer. . . . Summer passes, then autumn, and finally it is winter. The winter insects are a whole new breed and have perfected a new and revolutionary science on the basis of the 'hard facts' of their perception of snow. As for the myths and legends of summer: clearly, the intelligent insects are not going to believe the superstitions of their primitive ancestors." Wm. Irwin Thompson, *New York Times*, May 10, 1971.

There may be an all-or-none quality about such behavior which lends itself to the tendency to absolutism noted earlier. There may be an element of submissiveness or craving for being dominated that forms the basis for the cultic conformity we have observed. And a compulsive logorrhea may underlie the fanatic outpouring of one-way communication that accompanies missionary zeal. It is neither possible nor necessary here to pursue these conjectures much further than to suggest that there may be psychological and even physiological reasons (as well as cultural) why human beings caught up in intense meaning experiences sometimes behave in ways their neighbors find exasperating. Certain of these typical traits of intense meaning-behavior have been described in what has gone before, and the contention here is that *such behavior will continue,* and *will continue to exhibit these characteristic exasperating qualities.*

To express it in another way, all men need ultimate meaning—some more acutely than others and all at some periods of life more keenly than at others. Whenever and however and no matter by whom such urgent needs are felt, they tend to be satisfied through significance-seeking behavior that is partly dependent upon the culturally shaped meaning-bearing institutions of the given time and place, and partly upon certain intrinsic qualities of the intense meaning experience which are not derived entirely from culture patterns.

The Elemental Posture
of the Quest for Meaning

Foremost among the latter is a responsiveness to what I have called high demand. That is, the searcher recognizes meaning in part by what it costs him. He expects to have to pay dearly for the pearl of great price—in animal or human sacrifice, offerings of money or possessions, or self-commitment to celibacy, periodic temple-duty, full-time religious vocation, or various other forms of service, self-denial, or self-sacrifice. It is this quality of demand/

cost/commitment/investment that gives meaning its validation, its convincingness, its force. And it is precisely out of this essential quality that other, derivative qualities arise, some that are admirable and some that are abrasive. But because they seem to cluster together in the pattern described earlier—(1) Commitment/ (2) Discipline / (3) Missionary Zeal / (4) Absolutism / (5) Conformity / (6) Fanaticism—it is more appropriate to think of the syndrome as a whole, to appreciate its role in the generation and propagation of ultimate meaning, and to recognize that it is necessarily *both* admirable and abrasive.

The mechanism of commitment is such that it is commitment to a *particular* explanation or formulation of meaning and to the stream of collective experience or religious organization that bears it. In its most intense and typical form it is a total, undifferentiated, and unreserved attachment. Its dilute or degenerate counterfeit is an allegiance that is partial, ambivalent, or distributed among various competing objects—which is not commitment but its *opposite*: lukewarmness. It is the particularity of intense commitment that creates absolutism; that is, commitment to one particular faith and "against" all others. Whether or not such exclusiveness is *logically* necessary, it may be *psychologically* forceful and difficult to modify.

Commitment to a particular system of meaning also seems to entail submission to its authority, both in the admirable sense of accepting the group's discipline and in the exasperating sense of expecting and enforcing conformity, uniformity, submissiveness in other members of the group. Perhaps commitment does not *logically* require such behavior, but *psychologically* it seems to have that effect.

These qualities may be a by-product of the resistance which high-demand meaning-systems generate around them. Their usual pariah status seems to draw the members of such movements more closely together, intensifying their need for complete identification with the group, even to the displaying of badges of belonging which ensure and accentuate their ostracism from the rest of society. Thus compacted into a close-knit company by social pressures, the members may feel their investment of self in the group threatened by other members who break ranks in even the most trivial nonconformity.

Or it may be that the craving for meaning, the dread of normlessness or anomie, drives those who experience it to a rigid and uncritical embracing of meaning when they find it. Part of the commitment which some formulations of meaning demand of adherents is conformity to a specified or normative - pattern of thinking, feeling, and acting. When one adherent commits himself to that prescribed pattern, he expects others to do the same. If they do not appear to do so, he feels his own investment threatened. The greater that investment the greater the threat, and the greater his minatory rigor toward defaulters.

Commitment to a high-demand meaning movement also seems to produce a missionary zeal, a warmth and eagerness to share the newfound meaning with others, which can be admirable. But usually combined with it is a single-minded fanaticism unreceptive to differing views or alternative meanings, which can be obnoxious. Perhaps commitment does not *logically* require a refusal to consider sympathetically any meanings other than one's own, but *psychologically* it involves contortion to try to weigh impartially one set of views while clinging firmly to another. It is like the isotonic system of exercising that exerts one set of muscles against another: it may be possible, but it isn't easy.

Meaning-Commitment v. Dialogue

Dialogue among exponents of differing convictions can be an enriching experience, but it is a different kind and level of experience from that sought and appreciated by the person who has been desperately craving meaning and has just found it. Some have observed that converts are notoriously unreceptive to views which might shake their new faith, or that they seem to recite their beliefs so volubly partly to convince themselves. Those are negative ways of explaining that a person who has found new meaning for his life is understandably full of it, overflowing with it, and not much interested in anything else, especially not in speculating about alternative answers that might relativize his own.

Dialogue has been a profoundly beneficial experience for me. I have urged and advocated it for years, particularly between Christians and Jews, and have written, in collaboration with another enthusiast, a manual of instruction for it.[3] I have felt impatience with those Christian fundamentalists and Orthodox Jews who resist the obvious attractions of sharing theological discourse. Yet those who disdain or distrust it (among Christians, at least) are those whose religious groups are growing, while those who engage in it are the ones whose religious organizations are shrinking. So is dialogue a good thing or not?

The answer seems to be that it is good for some things and not for others. It is a mode of person-to-person communication whereby we can exchange in nondefensive sincerity our deepest convictions about the meaning of life and in the process come close to knowing the true personhood of those who hold differing convictions. It is an encounter between an "I" and a "thou," in Buber's terms,[4] rather than treating others as an "it" to be talked around or at, and is therefore the highest and most precious level of human communication. Even the ultimate meanings exchanged in theological dialogue, valuable as they are to the individuals involved and essential as they are to the whole human pilgrimage, are artifacts—"its"—of instrumental or derivative worth compared to persons.

Dialogue is a risk. Though one's convictions are often deepened and enriched rather than lost or changed, through dialogue one risks not only their alteration but the exposure of self to influence and modification. Yet it is only by risking our own most precious meanings that we are able to encounter the real person behind the façade which each of us uses to shield himself from the world. A person who has recently been—or still is—in an acute quest for meaning and has just caught hold of a "sacred cosmos" he can

---

3. Dean M. Kelley and Bernhard E. Olson, *The Meaning and Conduct of Dialogue* (New York: National Conference of Christians and Jews, 1970).
4. Martin Buber, *I and Thou* (New York: Charles Scribner's Sons, 1958).

cling to, is not apt to risk it by exposing its possible vulnerabilities to examination. On the other hand, one who is more secure in his sense of the meaningfulness of life—who has not recently passed through a meaning-void which leaves him shaken—may be more willing to venture an intimate exchange in which the most precious meanings are given an instrumental role as a means for encountering other persons.

Dialogue may be good for deepening the encounter of persons across the barriers that divide them, particularly the formidable barriers of religious differences, but it is not necessarily good for the systems of ultimate meaning on which those barriers are based. In fact, our evidence indicates, it is probably "bad" for meaning-systems to have their barriers crossed in such cavalier fashion. They are built at great cost in human commitment, as we have seen, for the purpose of generating, embodying, and protecting meaning—a crucial but specialized function. They remain strong and vigorous as long as that meaning is central and ultimate in their adherents' lives, as long as it provides the final test of worth and validity. So long as the faithful divide the righteous from the infidel on the basis of acceptance or rejection of a particular formulation of meaning, just so long will the faithful be willing to live and die for that meaning and the religious organization that bears and embodies it. When the merit of men and their works is not determined solely or exclusively by identification with that meaning-system but by other criteria as well, then that meaning-system cannot command the same degree of priority.

Either Meaning Is Important or It Isn't

To some this generalization may seem so obvious as to be almost circular, yet it is apparently a source of great confusion and misunderstanding to others, so let us approach it in another way. Much of the conflict, hatred, and misery of human history has arisen from ideological causes. That is, men have divided themselves into factions, parties, sects, and armies over issues of *faith* (religious or quasi-religious meanings) and have persecuted and slaughtered those whose faith was different from their own. Though this degree of fervor for meaning is brutal, bloody, and probably excessive, it is indicative of the elemental nature of the need for meaning and of the fierceness that threats to it can unleash. Also it suggests the single-minded fanatical devotion which the struggle for meaning and the defense of a meaning-system require—or at least evoke.

If meaning is to be central and ultimate, it will take precedence over all other things, including persons. If it does not take precedence over other things, including persons, it will no longer be central and ultimate. When it is no longer central and ultimate, meaning will be vulnerable to compromise, "balancing," trade-offs, dilution, lip-service, apathy, and neglect in relation to other values and considerations, and the meaning-system will proportionately recede in importance. That is what we are seeing happen to religion and churches today. Enlightened men have become wary (with good reason) of ideological causes, holy crusades—struggles for meaning in which persons are hurt. They have asked themselves whether *any* abstraction—particularly an abstraction that seems largely speculative—is worth one person's pain. Eschewing such fierce, rigid, single-value, and inhumane behavior, they no longer view meaning as something to die for. Attachments to meaning have thus become tenuous and tentative, meaning-systems marginal and then dispensable.

Meanwhile there are signs in our enlightened day of a growing famine of meaning, producing more than one person's pain, and the few who recognize what is lacking wonder where it was lost. It has not been just a failure of the predominant meaning-systems (though they have become effete and ineffectual, as already noted), but a double misreading of the entire meaning-producing and maintaining process in human history: (1) the erroneous assumption/conclusion that the vicious excesses of meaning-conflict in the past are necessary or inevitable, and (2) the failure to recognize that—even without such barbaric overkill—the pursuit of meaning is still essentially a fierce, imperious, single-minded, and elemental activity, not always indulgent of error or patient with backsliding. In overcorrecting for the excesses of the past, we have reduced the meaning-generating function to placidity, decorum, and tolerance—i.e., sterility—depriving it of the fierce, exclusivist, either/or asperities that are in some degree essential to it.

Those religious bodies which have preserved such qualities continue to thrive, though they offer only a very narrow spectrum of religious experience and terminology. It is possible to imagine a broad spectrum of religious expression and explanation, with many more formulations of meaning than are presently available, each validated and fortified by the kind of seriousness described earlier—yet without excesses of harshness—reaching millions more meaning-hungry people with an "explanation" that makes sense of life.

But even at their best, meaning enterprises are highly specialized in function. Their business is significance and everything else is subordinated to it. As with any goal-seeking activity, the greater the concentraton upon the goal, the greater the likelihood of success. To the extent that effort and attention are diffused, diverted to other objectives, or dissipated in self-defeating exertions, to that extent the activity becomes ineffective. Yet *man* is not specialized in function; he needs the ministrations of various functional institutions: economic, familial, governmental, recreational, etc. Sometimes he needs one and at other times another; rare is the person who can confine himself continuously to one interest or institution. When a person's need for meaning is intense, he can become almost completely occupied with the search for it and its appropriation and expression. For some people it may become a lifelong preoccupation: these are the virtuosi of religion—the saints and prophets. They keep the mills of meaning operating, and whoever enters the mill or needs its product must be prepared to follow its regimen.

Can Meaning Survive in Moderation?

Nevertheless, most people do not become perpetual devotees of a meaning regimen; their need for ultimate meaning is succeeded by other needs and interests, and their attention to the meaning-system wanes. They may maintain a routinized relationship with it (average church membership), but it no longer occupies their entire horizon: it recedes to a tenth or a hundredth part of what it was. And we have speculated that meaning-systems cannot be sustained at an effective level—certainly cannot be brought into being—by such partial, casual, and tepid adherence.

Most people, most of the time, consider someone else's obsession with any one interest, concern, or activity a cause for suspicion and uneasiness. They are inclined to look with distaste or positive aversion upon anyone who is too intense about anything—particularly religion. Yet they want the meaning-system available when they need it, failing to realize that it may not be able to serve their need without a greater investment of themselves in it. Ultimate meaning that no one is any longer giving his life for may no longer be very persuasive or convincing, even to those who claim to subscribe to it. So we are confronted with a dilemma which this chapter has sought to characterize in such a way that neither of its horns is blunted.

On the one hand, ultimate meaning is essential to human life, and it is effective to the degree that it demands and secures a central commitment in men's lives. Yet on the other hand, to attain that central significance, it often rides roughshod over other interests and values, sometimes even disregarding human well-being. Though the paradox can be reduced, it cannot be eliminated without being unfair to one pole or the other. There is about any serious meaning venture a certain irreducible fierceness, asperity, insistence, exclusiveness, rigor—a fanaticism that brushes everything else aside. Yet that very single-mindedness renders it objectionable to those who value balance, brotherhood, respect for individual diversity, mutual forbearance and self-restraint, civic peace, pluralism—and dialogue—as much as, or more than, they value any single formulation of meaning or any one meaning-system (including their own).

This dilemma is felt most sharply by those Christian church leaders who are committed both to the ultimate meaning embodied in the Christian faith and also to other human goals and values that are as important a part of life as ultimate meaning: freedom, justice, beauty, (empirical) truth, and respect for others—including those who are deeply devoted to non-Christian ultimate meanings, or to none at all. But why must there be any conflict? Are not freedom, justice, respect for others essential *parts* of the Christian faith? Ideally they should be, if rightly understood. One can conceive of a high-demand religious movement devoted to justice, freedom, beauty, respect for others, and so on, which could effectively explain life to men without fanaticism, absolutism, intolerance, or judgmental moralism. That is what—ideally— Christianity ought to be.

Yet where is such a phenomenon to be found? Even the most gentle, humble, and loving Christians must divide the world into those who confess Christ as Lord and those who don't. Of course, such a conceptual division is in itself not offensive (or is it?), so much as the consequences that flow from it: how are the former treated differently from the latter? If the Lordship of Christ, or any other threshold test of a meaning-system, is to have any validity, it must separate those who belong from those who do not in some significant ways, the essential minimum of which is membership in and control of the faith-group itself. From that basic distinction others are derived: those who accept the Lordship of Christ will act differently from those who do not; they will do certain things (virtues) which the others do not do; they will not do certain things (sins) which the others do; they will dress as well as act differently; and so on.

The more vivid and fervent the meaning-experience (i.e., the more effective it is as meaning), the more it will tend to dominate and pervade and overflow the believer's life. The effects of that process seem to emerge in the qualities of strictness we have examined earlier. Yet if those qualities are consciously eschewed or unconsciously avoided in order not to appear overintense, irrational, inconsiderate, offensive, exclusive, or fanatical, then the salience, the dominance, the effectiveness of the ultimate meaning seem to be eroded.

Is there no way to escape this dilemma? That depends upon

its cause. We have noted that many of the most violent excesses of meaning-conflict could probably be eliminated, but there may still be elements that are inseparable from the effective experience of meaning. As long as human beings who have found new meaning for their lives *show* it by new and different ways of speaking and acting, they are probably going to stir resistances, resentments, and animosities in their unchanged neighbors, who in turn will begin to avoid, taunt, mimic, insult, attack, and/or expel them. This rejecting behavior only makes the problem worse by intensifying the solidarity of the meaning-group and reinforcing its members' determination to persevere in whatever behavior they believe their faith requires.

The only way to avoid this outcome is to conceal the acquisition of meaning, to meet clandestinely (since meaning-experience is at some point a collective undertaking) and counterfeit the continuance of the old way of life—probably one of the hardest things for a human being to do. That way lie cloisters and catacombs, neither of which has been an ideal means of infusing the needed meaning into society at large or of reaching all persons who might respond to it but do not know they would until they are—at first exposure "offensively"—confronted by it.

Meaning and Religious Liberty

At best, the dilemma can only be minimized, not eliminated, by the restraint, tolerance, and indulgence which were the difficult but valued achievement of the Enlightenment. While "a little persecution" may be a remarkable tonic for the social strength of religious movements, it also accentuates the victim posture that deepens and perpetuates persecution; it aggravates the more paranoid forms of chosen-peoplehood: fear and rejection of non-believers, the stigmata of belonging, cryptic and symbolic code-language, and so forth. Persecution makes it more difficult for the group to work out and express its hard-won meanings free of trauma and distortion.

The modern ideal of religious liberty—that no one should be

persecuted or penalized for what he believes—recognizes and respects not only the dignity of all men but the preciousness to them of the ultimate meanings they have found. The ultimate meanings are valuable to them and therefore to everyone, since the man for whom life doesn't make sense (whether conventionally religious sense or not) is a potential hazard to himself and others. Religious liberty permits every person to promulgate his particular formulation of ultimate meaning without persecution (and therefore without some of the distortions persecution causes), thus maximizing the possibility that that meaning will resonate with the need of some meaning-hungry persons who might not otherwise find an explanation of existence suited to their several conditions and experiences. Thus it is not only for the unburdening of the would-be individual evangelist that religious liberty is a boon, but for enriching the mix of available meanings in the whole society, from which we all—directly or indirectly—benefit.

In addition to its philosophical and theological justifications, which we need not examine here, religious liberty is a profoundly pragmatic "article of peace"[5] designed to avoid the historic wars of religion. As Mr. Justice Black observed in writing the opinion of the U.S. Supreme Court in *Everson* v. *Board of Education*:

> With the power of government supporting them, at various times and places, Catholics had persecuted Protestants, Protestants had persecuted Catholics, Protestants sects had persecuted other Protestant sects, Catholics of one shade of belief had persecuted Catholics of another shade of belief, and all of these had from time to time persecuted Jews. In efforts to force loyalty to whatever religious group happened to be on top and in league with the government of a particular time and place, men and women had been fined, cast in jail, cruelly tortured, and killed. . . . The people [of Virginia], as elsewhere, reached the conviction that individual religious liberty could be achieved best under a government which was stripped of all power to tax, to support, or otherwise to assist any or all religion, or to interfere with the beliefs of any religious individual or group.[6]

5. John Courtney Murray, S. J., *We Hold These Truths* (New York: Sheed of Ward, 1960), p. 48.
6. Joseph Tussman, *The Supreme Court on Church and State* (New York: Oxford University Press, 1962), pp. 208, 209.

It is precisely because of the inherent fierceness of religious conflict that governments have learned, by sad and bitter experience, to handle it with utmost gingerliness. The Elizabethan Settlement introduced a novel though qualified toleration to end the alternating persecutions by Protestant and Catholic monarchs, a toleration that was gradually broadened and extended until it became a general recognition of men's rights to differ in religion. Religious liberty is the only peaceable way to deal with an area of human behavior that is both indispensable and potentially explosive.

But it must be a quality of religious liberty that moves beyond the Enlightenment view that all religious convictions are false or futile and therefore may be indulged. It must recognize that precisely because they can and do make a difference in men's lives, religious convictions must be respected and protected. And the convictions and organizations that are the most obnoxious and obstinate, exclusivist, and fanatical are the very ones that are the most effective in reaching the outcasts and outlaws who most need to find meaning for their lives. Thus the groups hardest to tolerate are the very ones that deserve it most.

It is not difficult to bear the mild and placid ministrations of the respectable churches, but these are not the ones that are redeeming habitual criminals and drug addicts in our society. It is the Black Muslims, the Jehovah's Witnesses, and the like that are doing it, and they are threatened and castigated, accused of being political rather than religious, preaching hatred and violence rather than virtue and love, stirring up dissension rather than promulgating peace, etc. Yet what is the *product* of this nefarious behavior? It is lives restored to self-respect, peaceableness, and self-discipline, families recovered for stability and self-determination, whole companies of men and women bound together and lifted up out of despair into mutual regard and reinforcement in the practice of meaningful, purposeful living.

In fact, their behavior (not their rhetoric) bears a striking resemblance to the old white, middle-class puritan morality which is so easy to criticize and so hard to replace with other qualities as conducive to reliability, productiveness, and integrity in human affairs. Elijah Muhammed's idiom may be Islam, but his model works more like Calvinism! Far from being an escape from reality, it enables its adherents together to begin to *cope* with reality in a constructive and dignified and peaceful way such as many of them were unable to aspire to before they were caught up in the movement that seems so repellent and nonsensical to outsiders.

The Black Muslims are a perfect example of a high-demand movement going its abrasive way and making life meaningful for thousands no other cure seems able to reach. Yet every issue of the *Ecclesiastical Court Digest* seems to report a case in which a warden somewhere is begrudging prisoners access to the Koran or a copy of *Muhammed Speaks* or a pork-free diet or a Muslim chaplain, often on the ground that their aspirations are political rather than religious. Let him who has as good a record of preventing recidivism as the Black Muslims refuse their requests! To judge by results, we could do worse than to give the Muslims all the access to prisons they want, supply them all the Korans and pork-free diets they can use, and pay them to make as many converts as they can. The only difficulty is that people do not become Black Muslims or preach its message for pay, and if they did accept such emoluments, they would lose a proportionate measure of convincingness to the very outlaws and outcasts they have been so unusually effective in reaching. This is another illustration of the point that, to some significant degree, *the very qualities that make a religious movement objectionable to critical outsiders are what make it convincing to adherents and potential converts.*

Persons v. Principles

The dilemma between intensity and civility, between fanaticism and humaneness, reflects a tension in human affairs (and indeed within each human being) between principle and regard for persons. The stern father portrayed in many a cartoon wrathfully driving his wayward daughter with her illegitimate baby out of the shamed parental home into the storm is a rigid, judgmental, ideology-driven, "inner-directed" figure of fun to his "other-directed,"[7] nonrigid, nonjudgmental, non-ideology-driven successors. What father in our generation would view such rejection, even in less cruel form, as the way to deal with a daughter's failure? What principle of right and wrong would loom larger on his horizon than the possibility of helping his daughter to rebuild life after what was at worst a damaging but all-too-human mistake? Would she not already have suffered enough from the disappointment of her hopes, the deception of her trust, the disruption of her affection, without suffering parental condemnation for violation of the Seventh Commandment as well? That is the sensible attitude to take, as we view it today. It is only a coincidence that the rates of illegitimacy, venereal disease, and other symptoms of social disorganization are increasing. Or *is* it?

The example chosen is extreme and so will doubtless lead to misunderstanding. It is not cited to suggest that the increase in illegitimacy is caused solely or mainly by fathers not fulminating sufficiently against fornication; there are many and complex causes of which this can be at most a minor one. Nor is it to suggest that judgmental moralism is the best or only way to deal with social disorganization, or that concern for persons is less important than devotion to principle. The inner-directed way of handling life is out of phase now, and I could no more subordinate persons to principles than could the average reader. As a result, both persons and principles may suffer.

One of the needs of at least some of our contemporaries is for more structured lives: state hospitals are crowded with children and adolescents with weak ego boundaries, who feel insecure and frightened because they do not know what the world expects of them or what they can expect of the world. All of us experience this to some extent: we feel ourselves adrift in a shapeless, borderless, unpredictable world, and we seek asylum from this intolerable condition. If we do not find asylum in a shared world of meaning that gives shape and significance to existence, we may seek it desperately in more destructive and less satisfying ways, including that to which the word *asylum* more specifically applies.

7. Two now classic types portrayed in David Riesman's *The Lonely Crowd* (New Haven: Yale University Press, 1950).

The Alternation of
Regularization and Relaxation

The shared world of human meaning varies in its intensity and forcefulness from time to time and place to place. Diverse influences, such as rapid social change or intercultural diffusion, may cause it to fade, distort, or shatter. It can be restored or replaced by a new world only through a large-scale collective enterprise, a shift from individualized dispersion, diversity, and heterogeneity to a new consolidation of social cohesion, expectation, and homogeneity. Such shifts are often, perhaps usually, brought about by a resurgence of vigor in the religious realm, a reassertion of the collective moral expectations of society, a restrictiveness toward nonconformity—qualities, on a large and secular, society-wide scale, that we have observed within vigorous religious movements and organizations. This is the *re*organization by which societies pull themselves together after periods of disorganization.

A Cromwellian era of moralistic rigor and religious fervor is followed by a Restoration era of licentiousness and laxity. A Wesleyan revival can call to the hunger for structure, for regularization, for predictability, for an end to cynicism and excess in a whole society. It is not due just to the persuasiveness of the preachers in making converts; they are often the beneficiaries of tides of readiness for a reassertion of structure. We are feeling some of that type of readiness today, as people grow tired of change and fearful of unrest. They want the world to settle down and hold still awhile until they get it all sorted out again. If this yearning persists, it may lead to a rigorous restructuring that could bring us out of our present phase of major preoccupation with persons into one of primary concern for principles—the obverse side of which is a repression of dissent and nonconformity in the name of law-and-order (a principle for which many persons have been made to suffer).

There is an alternation, an ebb and flow, between rigidification and relaxation, between consolidation and divergence. It is difficult to predict the period of such tides since they are a complex confluence of many pressures and rhythms, long and short, global and local. Far from attempting to measure or predict, all that is attempted here is to point out motion in one direction followed by motion in the other, and to suggest that each has its merits and defects and neither should be despised.

Just as the sublimation of sexual energy into more complex, permanent, and creative outcomes is dependent upon restraints that focus and conserve as well as inhibit its expression, so many of the more lasting, constructive collective achievements of human effort have been made possible by constriction, delay, and redirection imposed in periods of rigidity of social expectations (emphasis on principles). Though painful and frustrating, in such structures the pressures of human energy build up until they reach a higher and more sublimated level of release. Put conversely, an era in which individuals are encouraged and enabled to find many easy and short-term gratifications will be one in which not many will discover the need to achieve anything requiring patience or persistence, postponement of gratification, acceptance of punishment, endurance of pain, overcoming of failure and disappointment, sharing or relinquishment of rewards to others, etc.—qualities that have marked history's more memorable periods of achievement.

It takes more energy to enforce a set of rules or principles for conduct, to keep account, to reward, admonish, and punish than it does to let it go. That expenditure of energy on behalf of abstractions and at the cost of considerable interpersonal friction is the fruit and further seeding of a season of structuring and stressing, as standards of human conduct are raised, rigidified, enforced, and reinforced. It is a stern and judgmental season, when people say to one another, "Shape up or ship out" and other ungracious things.

The point is that, though it may be an arduous era, it is no less a *human* one. Cromwell and Cotton Mather are as characteristic of the race as Charles II and Rousseau. If anything, we may suspect that the periods of principle are those of human progress,[8] while those of humaneness are intervals of rest. We would not be where we are now (and it is not all to our discredit) were it not for waves of ancestors fiercely determined about their principles alternating with waves that were more solicitous of human well-being, irrespective of abstractions. We should not be surprised that men can sometimes be rather grim about what they believe at the expense of those they love, and it is not a bad thing that this is so.

Thus in society as a whole, as well as in meaning-seeking-and-maintaining groups (religious organizations) and individuals, we see a tension, sometimes an alternation, between the urge to tighten up toward envisioned collective objectives and the propensity for letting down toward individual autonomy and diversity. Because it is presently out of phase, I have given more attention here to the tightening-up process, to induce the rueful recognition that it serves an essential function in human society, uncongenial as it may be at the present moment. If the advocates of maximizing individual autonomy and diversity (of whom in many respects I am one) can ever show that such a state is stable—and the present situation scarcely demonstrates this—perhaps we might dispense with the astringent process. Some day it may be possible. But there are sufficient symptoms of increasing social and personal anomie, or meaninglessness, to suggest that the letting-down end of the continuum is not an adequate permanent arrangement. Each phase has its benefits and excesses, but mankind needs both. We have examined the mechanisms of the tightening-up phase to gain a better appreciation of its benefits and suggest ways to mitigate its excesses. To maximize the former and minimize the latter, we must develop ways of preserving principles without harming persons. At the same time, we must learn to respect the strictness, the seriousness, the severity which the maintenance of meaning in human life requires.

8. This word has been a battleground, and I do not mean to take sides in that controversy or to imply that progress is inevitable; I merely suggest by it periods of successfully assimilated innovation by means of which a level of increasing complexity and awareness is attained, the effects of which are invariably bad as well as good.

Summary and Conclusions

Human beings cannot live without trying to make sense of their experience, to find the meaning in it. When they discover a broad explanation that satisfies them, they are shielded by it from dejection and dread. The same answer will not work for everyone, and some are more satisfying than others. Most such explanations originate with a religious group, since their convincingness and continuity derive from the commitment given to them by a community of devotees. These communities begin as high-demand religious or quasi-religious movements capable of changing the lives of men and the course of history. As the level of demand decreases, they "run down" and decline in social strength and numbers until they reach a state of minimal activity, which may continue for centuries.

This process of decline can be delayed—though probably not reversed—by the exercise of "strictness," which is the consequence and evidence of the seriousness of meaning. Even from declining religious groups many people derive what meaning they have; for some it may be all they need. And from declining groups new movements spring, which may lend vitality to the old or may begin a new evolution or both.

Strictness has led to grievous excesses in the past (such as crusades and inquisitions), which should remind us that the pursuit of meaning is serious business and can become dangerous. Without such seriousness, however, the meaning-quest becomes lax and desultory—which can also be dangerous, since a failure of meaning may have a destructive effect on society as well as on individuals.

We are living in a day when strictness is out of favor, and the qualities which are popularly esteemed in religious groups are those that conduce, not to the strength of the quest for meaning, but to its weakening: relativism, diversity, dialogue—leniency. What are the implications of this situation for the major Protestant denominations? If a religious group—old or new—wants to keep from dying, how should it proceed?

Implications for the Ecumenical Churches

To the person who is concerned about the future of the ecumenical churches, this theory can offer little encouragement. The mainline denominations will continue to exist on a diminishing scale for decades, perhaps for centuries, and will continue to supply some people with a dilute and undemanding form of meaning, which may be all they want. These dwindling denominations may spawn new movements which, if they pursue the hard road of strictness, may have vital effects on human life, such as the declining churches had in their youth but can no longer achieve.

The plans for the amalgamation of the chief ecumenical churches into one body—the "Church of Christ Uniting"—and hopes for a really inclusive National Conference of Churches or a worldwide parliament of all religions, all are symptoms and confirmations of the process of relaxation described in this book. Such ecumenical endeavors may be conducive to brotherhood, peace, justice, freedom, and compassion, but they are not conducive to conserving or increasing the social strength of the religious groups involved or—more important—the efficacy of the ultimate meanings which they bear.

Conserving Strength in an Adverse Era

Suppose a pastor or a layman in one of the ecumenical denominations wanted to strengthen the congregation of which he was a part. How would he go about it? Abundant suggestions may be found in the foregoing material, especially in Chapter VIII. To begin with, he might try to put into effect the "Minimal Maxims of Seriousness" listed on p. 121. It will do no harm to review them concisely here.

1. Those who are serious about their faith do not confuse it with other beliefs, loyalties, or practices, or mingle them together indiscriminately, or pretend they are alike, of equal merit, or mutually compatible if they are not.
2. Those who are serious about their faith make high demands of those admitted to the organization that bears the faith, and they do not include or allow to continue within it those who are not fully committed to it.
3. Those who are serious about their faith do not consent to, encourage, or indulge any violations of its standards of belief or behavior by its professed adherents.
4. Those who are serious about their faith do not keep silent about it, apologize for it, or let it be treated as though it made no difference, or should make no difference, in their behavior or their relationships with others.

In the same chapter (pp. 125–127), the ways in which Anabaptists and Wesleyans tried to put such seriousness into effect were summarized, and might be generalized as follows:

a. Be in no haste to admit members.
b. Test the readiness and preparation of would-be members.
c. Require continuing faithfulness.
d. Bear one another up in small groups.
e. Do not yield control to outsiders, nor seek to accommodate to their expectations.

Perhaps the initial and essential step in all this is for the members of the congregation to determine what ultimate meanings they are going to embrace and embody. If as a whole they are not ready to do so, perhaps it will be necessary to begin with a nucleus of those who are, and organize them into a discipleship group (an *ecclesiola*) to which others in time may be attracted. This will not be easy, and the dangers of elitism will need to be guarded against. Still, there will be in every congregation some who *want* to be called to a really serious discipleship.

This tactic has been used many times in many places; sometimes it results in schism, sometimes in revitalization of the church. Often the degree of new seriousness is not sufficient to withstand the inertia of the congregation, and the effort soon collapses. Sometimes it is "domesticated" by the congregation, its challenge tamed, contained, and channeled to some limited objective such as visiting the sick or greeting new members. Sometimes it is distracted by or diverted to some too-large objective which does not clearly communicate ultimate meaning, such as a campaign for open housing or world peace. This does not mean that such activities are always inappropriate or may never be the expression of ultimate meaning; their appropriateness has to do with the meaning to be conveyed and their proportion to the group's energies: an aim is overbroad whose sheer logistical demands would devour all the time and effort of the group without producing visible results or effective communication of ultimate significance. The meaning which the *ecclesiola* tries to embody and express may be radical or conservative from the standpoint of the world. There is no reason why the group could not preach and practice radical and voluntary poverty or pacifism if it desires. In fact, the more radical the meaning, the higher the demand upon members who embody it, and the stronger the group will consequently be. But whatever the final meaning to be expressed and embodied, the group must be thoroughly and uncompromisingly committed to it.

The same principles apply in the organization of a new group outside existing traditions. Any commune, for instance, seeking to survive its first winter would be well-advised to determine what it is trying to accomplish, distill its purposes into brief compass, and eliminate everything that distracts or detracts from them. This does not necessarily mean drawing up a creed or a set of rules and regulations; the Anabaptists never had either, but they hammered out—by costly trial and error—a fairly clear stance and attitude, so that it became readily apparent who belonged to the group and who did not.

Both new groups and old must find an effective yet humane way to exercise the only power a voluntary group possesses to preserve its integrity: the power of the gate. They must be willing and ready to exclude those who do not measure up to the group's standards, whatever those may be. Many groups have high and admirable standards, but when it comes to enforcing them against specific offenders, they lack the will—the seriousness—to do so. It is not necessary to be cruel or harsh about such enforcement, nor to condemn the offender as worthless or abhorrent. He has simply failed to meet the qualifications of the group and is therefore no longer a member; it is as simple as that, but must not be blurred or glossed over.

In or *out*: upon this distinction the survival of any serious group depends. If it fails to separate out those who are not in earnest about its purposes, it may go on—for a while—as a group, but its real purposes do not go on. They will deteriorate quickly under such neglect, and so eventually will the group itself.

Groups which preserve their seriousness through strictness will not only mediate effective meaning to their members and others, but as a consequence will thrive and grow. Having avoided many forms of failure as well as having survived scorn, ridicule, and persecution, they will attain the eminence from which decline is certain—that is, success. As in other areas of life, the rewards of successful functioning often undermine the very qualities that produced it.

Strictness is not congenial to the prosperous, and so it ebbs away, and with it social strength.

Yet it should not be necessary for great meaning movements to throw away their strength by capitulating to the expectations of outsiders, by organizational promiscuity, by lowering of membership standards, and by loss of insistence on their seriousness. If this book has cast some light on the critical importance of meaning in human affairs—how it is engendered, propagated, and appropriated, and how organizations can serve the cause of meaning with seriousness or betray it by leniency, indulgence, and inertia—it will have benefited the churches more than if it were devoted simply to their praise or blame.

Index